John Wesley's
52 Standard Sermons

John Wesley's 52 Standard Sermons

An Annotated Summary

John S. Knox

Foreword by Phil Towne
Afterword by David R. Leonard

WIPF & STOCK · Eugene, Oregon

JOHN WESLEY'S 52 STANDARD SERMONS
An Annotated Summary

Copyright © 2017 John S. Knox. All rights reserved. Except for brief quotations in critical publications or reviews, no part of this book may be reproduced in any manner without prior written permission from the publisher. Write: Permissions, Wipf and Stock Publishers, 199 W. 8th Ave., Suite 3, Eugene, OR 97401.

Wipf & Stock
An Imprint of Wipf and Stock Publishers
199 W. 8th Ave., Suite 3
Eugene, OR 97401

www.wipfandstock.com

PAPERBACK ISBN: 978-1-5326-0809-4
HARDCOVER ISBN: 978-1-5326-0811-7
EBOOK ISBN: 978-1-5326-0810-0

Manufactured in the U.S.A.   MARCH 15, 2017

This book is dedicated to my beloved students. It is comforting not to be alone, surrounded by friends, as we explore the deep ways of God together.

> I want to know one thing, the way to heaven—
> how to land safe on that happy shore.
> God himself has condescended to teach the way:
> for this very end he came from heaven.
> He hath written it down in a book. O give me that book!
> ... Let me be homo unius libri [a man of one book].
> Here then I am, far from the busy ways of men.
> I sit down alone: only God is here.
> In his presence I open, I read his Book;
> for this end, to find the way to heaven.
>
> —JOHN WESLEY[1]

---

1. Bartleby.com, "A Man of One Book."

Contents

Illustrations | viii
Foreword by Phil Towne | ix
Preface | xiii
Acknowledgments | xvii

1   Introduction to John Wesley, the Preacher | 1
2   The Life of John Wesley | 5
3   Annotated Sermon Summaries | 31
4   Theological Reflections | 76

Afterword by David R. Leonard | 85
Glossary | 87
Recommended Reading | 93
Bibliography | 95
52 Standard Sermons Topical Index | 99
General Index | 105

Illustrations

Figure 1: Timeline | 29
Figure 2: Map of the United Kingdom | 30

Foreword

AT MOST SEMINARIES, THERE are not many pastors as renown and celebrated as Rev. John Wesley, the founder of the Methodist movement (1703–1791). I remember first studying Wesley when I was in graduate school in Portland, Oregon. I had, of course, heard of the man prior to that, but when learning of his open-air preaching and his powerful "method" of small groups, I was instantly impressed and captivated by his character. After more serious reading and reflection on his standard sermons, I found them to be inspiring and refreshing, and still relevant today, somewhat surprisingly.

History tells us that Wesley viewed the entire world as his parish. It did not matter where he was at, geographically; rather, he believed that he was called to share the Good News whenever he was called. As a counter-point to the Calvinist perspective of his day, he was also a staunch Arminian,[1] which comes out clearly in the sermons provided in this book. God lets people make choices, and Wesley felt called to help them make good, holy ones.

Wesley's own personal story is an interesting one—although a well-trained and well established Christian pastor, when attending a Moravian meeting in 1738,[2] he experienced a turning point of his own that left his heart feeling "strangely warmed" in a way

1. Olsen, *The Story of Christian Theology*, 464.
2. Olsen, 510.

that allowed him to have full assurance of his own forgiveness of sins and salvation. It was soon after this epiphany that his sincere evangelism began with English Anglican George Whitefield and Wesley's brother, Charles, in collaboration and support.

Spiritual brothers in the "Holy Club,"[3] these three ministers are credited with helping launch the Great Awakening in England,[4] which spread to the American colonies in the 1730s–1740s. Their skills and gifts were well accepted by most who had the fortunate opportunity to hear them preach on salvation and sanctification. John Wesley, himself, was down-to-earth when speaking to the crowds, which contrasted greatly with the reserved and aloof "high church" approach held by most church leaders in his day. Wesley's style of ministry was driven by a theological perspective suggesting that salvation was for all people—not just a select few or the social elites. For Wesley, love multiplied, but hate divided.

Perhaps driving his generous spirituality, Wesley placed a very high (if not the highest) value on the Bible. Thus, you will find in his sermons a rich exposition of scripture, as well as a high authority placed on the *Holy Bible* for guiding society and morality, and for aiding in understanding the complicated (and sometimes corrupt) culture of his day. Wesley's sermons are not simple, but they are sublime.

With the aforementioned in mind, Dr. John S. Knox's *John Wesley's 52 Standard Sermons: An Annotated Summary* offers valuable guidance for pastors, scholars, and laypeople who might be teaching through some of the same scriptural passages that Wesley analyzes, or studying Wesley's sermons for inspiration in their own pastoral messages, or for others who simply want to immerse themselves in Wesleyan thought and philosophy. The summaries of sermons contained in Knox's book come from Wesley's best homilies—each one poignant and purposeful for promoting personal growth and inspiration. Perhaps like Wesley, readers will feel "strangely warmed" through the reading of these beautiful,

---

3. Gonzalez, "Wesley, John (1703–91)," 1483.
4. Olsen, 511.

FOREWORD

heart-felt words imploring us to draw nearer to God, to each other, to holiness, and to love.

Wesley played a crucial role in English and American church history, and pastors and theologians from all denominations are indebted to him for his amazing preaching and his provocative teachings. John S. Knox has done a service for pastor and parishioner alike by writing this helpful summary of Wesley's works—not just to intellectually unravel and understand the sermons of Wesley, but to also encourage readers to apply the great truths concerning the heart of God presented in scripture.

I pray a blessing for all readers as you read and use *John Wesley's 52 Standard Sermons: An Annotated Summary*.

Phil Towne
PhD, Fuller Theological Seminary
Director of SALT and Certificate Programs
Assistant Professor of Bible and Ministry
Hope International University

Preface

THE BEGINNINGS OF THIS book began nearly two decades ago (2001) at George Fox Seminary in an independent study course that I took on John Wesley, the father of the Methodist Movement. Having grown up in both Southern Baptist and Conservative Baptist churches, my understanding of Wesley, Arminianism, and Methodism was limited, to say the least, but having learned more about the man and his mission in my Christian History and Thought class, I felt my own heart yearning to understand more about Wesley (in fact, I would later write my Master's thesis on Jacobus Arminius and his *Declaration of Sentiments*, which helped me appreciate Wesley's 1765 article, "What is an Arminian?"). Thus, I began my study, reading all the primary and secondary works that I could get my hands on regarding this prestigious founder of that monumental movement in those few months.

My professor, Dr. Larry Shelton, had prescribed several important books for my "proper Wesleyan edification" including *Christianity According to the Wesleys: The Harris Franklin Rall Lectures, 1954* by Franz Hildebrandt (Baker, 1996), *Aldersgate Heritage* (Methodist Evangelistic Materials, 1964), *Scriptural Christianity: A Call to John Wesley's Disciples* by Robert Chiles (Francis Asbury, 1989), *John Wesley and Education* by Alfred Body (Epworth Press, 1936), Wesley's *A Plain Account of Christian Perfection* (Beacon Hill, 1966), and *Wesley's 52 Standard Sermons: as He Approved*

Them (Schmul, 1988), of course. I provided book reviews of the secondary sources and a reflection paper on *A Plain Account of Christian Perfection* (I find both primary and secondary works to be quite edifying; however, I always have enjoyed reading the source and coming up with my own conclusions). Additionally, I also presented my beloved professor an annotated summary of each of Wesley's 52 sermons.

I must say that the experience of reading Wesley's writings that summer was tumultuous, at times. Many of his theological assertions cut me to the bone; others had me scratching my head, wondering how Wesley could biblically support his view. Reading through *A Plain Account of Christian Perfection* the first time had me repeatedly yelling out, "Yes, yes! Wait, no! No!" However, wrestling with *Wesley's 52 Standard Sermons*, I was constantly impressed with the depth and sophistication of his messages. It made me wonder what Wesley would think of the quality of preaching going on today. His sermons were never meant to tickle the ear; they were intended to move the heart and stimulate the intellect, and that takes a strong, resolute message, but also one wrapped in mercy and charity.

As the Epistle of Jude says, we are to "Contend for the faith;" however, the Epistle to the Galatians also states, "Restore each other gently." It was easy to see Wesley trying to balance the two in his sermons. Nearly two decades later, I must admit I love to talk about Wesley and Pietism in my Church History courses; Wesley's personal approach fills me with hope in our postmodern, Sacro-Egoistical[1] world. Moreover, as Dunning remarks,

> The danger of authoritarianism is always with us in corporate life . . . On the other side, with no less of a reprehensible character, is the perversion of irresponsible individualism. Here one ignores corporate responsibilities and the essential ties with the people of God in order to 'do his own thing.' It may be, and usually is, as much a violation of agape as authoritarianism is.[2]

1. See Knox, *Sacro-Egoism*.
2. Dunning, 103.

Preface

Finally, Wesley's writings made me ponder what a debate between Wesley and John Piper (or Mark Driscoll or Brian McLaren or Rob Bell) would be like. I am not sure of the conclusion(s), but I know I would love to buy a ticket to see their exchanges.

Nevertheless, at the end of that summer independent study course, I presented the professor a portfolio of my work and he was pleased with my reviews and reflection, but he was especially interested in my summary of *Wesley's 52 Standard Sermons*, of which he asked to keep a copy. I think my professor assumed that I would simply use *Wesley's 52 Standard Sermons* as a reference text. Instead, I began to develop a quantitative and qualitative research paper on the lot, focusing on each of the sermons to increase my understanding of Wesley's ministerial and discipleship ideas. He must have informed my Christian History and Thought professor about my work because he also asked for a copy (among others in the department including the Dean).

On a lark (or perhaps because of Holy Spirit prompting) some years later, I decided to create a short e-pamphlet of my original report on Wesley's sermons, which I mentioned on my Facebook page. Soon thereafter, a Wesleyan scholar and friend at Oregon State University asked for a copy as well. With so much affirmation over the years, it seemed apparent that my thesis was provocative and resonant.

Of course, no one term paper can provide what I had sought to personally discover at seminary—a comprehensive, evidential study of Wesley and Wesleyanism that would allow for objective, fair appraisal. Thus, I decided to expand my thesis into a book and add in several components based on my previous research on Wesley that had aided in my own comprehension. Having discussed the project with a few friends, pastors, and peers, I then began my work in earnest.

I had three main goals in mind while developing my new manuscript. First, I wanted to provide a general summary of Wesley's life and theological beliefs to help those from other denominations and faiths unfamiliar with him who wanted to know more. Second, I wanted to provide a thorough analysis for church

Preface

historians and theologians concerning the content and context of his 52 sermons. Finally, I wanted to provide a handy resource for pastors, Wesleyan and others, to find—and unravel—Wesley's powerful messages of spiritual (re)formation and public philanthropy to aid in evangelism, sanctification, and piety.

At the end of this writing project, I am struck with a humble awareness that I could have written so much more about Wesley, gone into greater details about his understanding of Christian Perfection, Prevenient Grace, and the specifics of his efficacious methodology, his ministerial priorities, and application of the faith in greater society, etc. Yet, Wesley's career lasted nearly seventy years. There is no one (besides perhaps the prolific Karl Barth) who could possibly cover every aspect of Wesley in perfect detail in one book; however, I feel confident that Wesley would have appreciated my attempt to understand him more fully, to create a sense of sympathy regarding his trials and tribulations on his own path to sanctification, and to fairly explain his theological assertions, their justifications, and goals.

Of course, knowing Wesley, he would have warmly affirmed my pithy endeavor and then would have most likely also suggested that I had "a bit more work to do," but that it certainly could be accomplished through the grace and loving assistance of God (and with no work breaks to get me in trouble).

Acknowledgments

FIRST AND FOREMOST, I offer my sincerest gratitude to my former Wesleyan professor, Dr. Larry Shelton. While at George Fox Seminary, I had the distinct joy and honor of receiving proper Wesleyan edification from Dr. Shelton in several classes, chapel sermons, and guest lectures. I remember asking Larry if he would be willing to work with me in an independent study course on Wesley, and if memory serves, he replied, "John, how could I possibly say, 'No,' to teaching 'John Knox' about Wesleyanism." His in-depth understanding of Wesley, his overflowing generosity in sharing his wisdom and knowledge on Methodism and its founder, and his witty and cheeky sense of humor made our classes and my learning an enriching and inspirational experience. Were it not for his opening the door, I would have missed out on a priceless time of investigating and discovering the joys of Wesleyanism. Perhaps I should call him, "Prevenient Larry," from now on.

Additionally, I appreciate the editorial and proofing assistance during the final stages of writing by my brother, George (it is good to have a family member with a Masters in Literature); confidant, racquetball comrade, and local Nampa pastor, Keith; former George Fox University student and friend, Heather (who just earned her BA in Biblical Studies with a Literature Minor as I write this); and American History teacher, racquetball partner, and friend, Kristin Hughes. To one and all, if iron sharpens iron, your "sparks" were both welcome and beneficial. I continually found myself saying, "Oh, bravo! Good catch!" when reading through your editorial suggestions.

Finally, because of their generosity and expertise, I am also deeply indebted to both Dr. Phil Towne and Chaplain David Leonard for their erudite foreword and afterword contributions. This collaboration brought back such fond memories of our time together at George Fox Seminary (even though nearly two decades have passed). I still love our passionate dialogues and debates about the Christian faith and how to find greater closeness to God and each other. I am proud to call you friends and confidants; I am in good company, indeed.

Of course, I could not have completed this book without the on-going support and love of my wife, Brenda, and my very patient sons, Jacob and Joe. This is my third book in my academic career, and as with all my literary adventures, their graciousness and kindness is both exemplary and inspiring.

1

Introduction to John Wesley, the Preacher

SINCE THE EARLY DAYS of the faith, numerous theologians and scholars have presented from the pulpit and lecterns various interpretations and applications regarding true Christian behavior and thought. In the 1700s, one Anglican preacher—the future founder of the Methodist Church, John Wesley—provided his own ministerial summations of what it meant to him to be a healthy, authentic Christian, based upon his years of prayer, biblical analysis, theological studies, and ministerial experiences.

In his comprehensive writings and speeches, Wesley did not issue mere edicts for the devout Christian to follow. In the struggle for and (hopeful) attainment of perfection from the believer, he offered both biblical justification and personal incentives toward that goal; and in eighteenth-century England, the social scene was fertile soil for Wesley's notions of true Christianity. Alfred Body states, "There was a ready acceptance of society and life as divinely fixed, comfortably based on the difference in rank, and consequently in importance, of the various classes of mankind."[1]

Wesley, however, disliked the cynical, despotic assumption that spiritual life was to be mechanically and coldly controlled through the churches and schools in English society. With fervent hope, he followed " . . . his own consuming desire to spread

1. Body, *John Wesley and Education*, 18.

religion to all"[2]—regardless of social class or circumstances. Wesley "observed the poverty and misery of the poor, and his heart was stirred to give them a better existence."[3]

Ever the great, hopeful egalitarian, Wesley believed that, because all people were children of God, all people could experience joy and blessings from their faith. As Field asserts,

> However, he rejected the Calvinist solution that God chose some human beings to be saved and then through a special intervention of God's grace called these and only these out of sin, enabling them to repent and believe. Wesley argued that God loved all human beings; that Christ had died for the salvation of all, and God would not hold people responsible for not doing what they were incapable of doing . . . the spirit of God was present and active in all people creating within them the ability to respond to God.[4]

This idea is known as "Prevenient Grace" and it is not just an invention of Wesley's; other great theologians held similar beliefs such as Thomas Aquinas and Jacobus Arminius. Wesley discusses both grace and predestination further in his 128th sermon, titled "Free Grace."[5]

With this ongoing gift going before salvation, Wesley believed that for the sinner, once saved, "His [the Christian's] heart is lifted up to God at all times, and in all places."[6] Moreover, Wesley asserted, "Christians are saved in this world from all sin, from all unrighteousness; that they are now in such a sense perfect, as not to commit sin, and to be freed from evil thoughts and evil tempers."[7] The sadness and pointlessness of English life had a cure, according to Wesley, and that cure was rooted in a healthy, loving relationship with God and one's neighbor.

2. Ibid., 40.
3. Ibid., 133.
4. Field, "The Unrealized Ethical Potential," 2.
5. Wesley Center Online, "Free Grace."
6. Wesley, *A Plain Account of Christian Perfection*, 18.
7. Ibid., 27–28.

Introduction to John Wesley, the Preacher

Such Christian perfection was more than a theoretical possibility for Wesley. The true Christian's whole heart and mind should and could be so attuned to God that his or her will was ultimately God's to direct and develop—thus, enabling perfection in Christ-like thought and deed. This perfected Christian could be "all devoted," ready to live out the Great Commandment(s) of Jesus in the Gospels, with God's assistance, a willing heart, and a submissive, disciplined commitment to obey God and serve others. As Robert Chiles notes, "Wesley desired those called by God both to equip and to deport themselves so as to serve the community of the Spirit as effectively as possible."[8] Religion was not supposed to be about just social management for Wesley; it was about a relationship of grace—something he saw lacking in his own life (at times) and definitely in the lives and culture surrounding him.

Perhaps no greater resource for Wesley's ministerial furtherance of sanctification exists than the collections of his sermons that have been gathered together in various volumes in paper and digital form. As O'Brien notes, "It is worth noting that it is the Standard Sermons that are singled out from Wesley's many writings as having a level of special importance and that these focus on the dynamics of Christian experience."[9]

Within *Wesley's 52 Standard Sermons*,[10] it is possible to view a multitude of Wesley's sermons that were presented at Oxford, various parishes, and even from his field preaching with George Whitefield during the first Great Awakening in America. In his messages, readers encounter the honest heart, brilliant insights, and soul-searching of John Wesley, and can truly come to comprehend the origins and aspirations of his theological approach for the Faith.

Indubitably, Wesley had a variety of personal and contextual objectives for each sermon. Yet, over-arching ideas and themes can be ascertained in his variegated orations; however, as Vickers states, "To understand and appreciate John Wesley, it is imperative

---

8. Chiles, *Scriptural Christianity*, 89.
9. O'Brien, "John Wesley, the Uniting Church," 171.
10. Wesley, *Wesley's 52 Standard Sermons*.

to locate his life and work within the intellectual, social, and political context of England's long eighteenth century."[11] Thus, a brief biography, timeline, and theological overview will be provided of John Wesley. Though a lengthy booklet could easily be written on each sermon by itself, for the purposes of this book, the reader will be provided with a concise overall summary of what Wesley was trying to convey in his messages, specific key themes found within each sermon, as well as pivotal pronouncements from Wesley's pulpit for his congregations and hearers.

Not shy when it came to comprehensive expository discussion, the length of each sermon was close to ten pages, so there is a voluminous amount of pure Wesley exposition to examine. Franz Hildebrandt points out that Wesley felt, "The Word of God is sufficient to speak for itself and to see its own success."[12] Thus, Wesley did not need to invent new theology; what he read in the Bible was more than sufficient. Moreover, Wesley sincerely believed that his only duty or ability was "To invite, to convince; to offer Christ; to build up; and to do this in some measure in every sermon."[13] The foundation of all salvation, however, rested upon the Holy Spirit's influence and activity in the sinner's life.

The truths promulgated by the Reverend John Wesley in eighteenth-century England and America are just as pertinent in the present, amorphous, postmodern era as they were in his own turbulent life and culture. Some of this is due to the timelessness of Scriptural truths, but some of it can be attributed to the enthusiasm and productive aphorisms of Wesley's messages of faith for all believers. As Curtis remarks, "His legacy was not just limited to his century or country, but survives today in the faith of millions in a variety of churches."[14] Therefore, in examining these fifty-two standard sermons, it is best to be prepared for ministerial admonitions that both simultaneously stir the heart to repentance and challenge the will to holy obedience.

11. Vickers, "Wesley's Theological Emphases," 190.
12. Hildebrandt, *Christianity According to the Wesleys*, 55.
13. Ibid., 55.
14. Curtis, "Revival and Revolution," 34.

2

The Life of John Wesley

From Fire to Founder

To fully grasp the significance of *Wesley's* 52 *Standard Sermons*, it is crucial to examine the milieu surrounding the life journey of the founder of the Methodist Movement. Understanding the events and experiences of Wesley's childhood through his ministry years and into his final days allows a beneficial glimpse into the inner workings and influences of the man who touched so many lives and created a theological revolution in England and America.

Eighteenth-Century Life

Culturally, rural and urban life up to the eighteenth-century in England had relatively stayed the same for centuries. English society centered on the family unit; one could expect to find father, mother, children, (and servants if wealthy enough) in a typical English home. Duties were generally assigned per gender; men tended to do the bulk of the agricultural and heavy labor; save perhaps at harvest, most women focused on domestic duties, which could be no small task considering the size and complications of families at that time. In rural England, life expectancy was not that great in the villages, with most people typically just making it to middle age. In the bigger cities, life expectancy was higher—especially if one's social status and benefits were higher and richer.

The serenity (or stagnation) of this social scene changed, dramatically, with the advent of the early Industrial Revolution (1760–1840). Halliday writes,

> Thus, though the wealth of the few was multiplying, the poverty and misery of the many, unprotected by the state, deprived of the means of production, and driven to live in slums and work appallingly long hours for pitifully low wages in factories and mines, young children as well as men and women, were increasing equally rapidly.[1]

The Industrial culture quickly supplanted the family unit as the central focus of life for many in England. The demand for new and better products skyrocketed, manufacturing plants were erected all over the country, and privately funded cities were constructed nearly overnight around these manufacturing regions. These plants needed workers of all sizes and genders, so soon the traditional family structure and routine were overridden by the company schedule and demands. Without mothers and fathers at home to teach their children (or children at home to learn from their parents), the illiteracy rate rose, with only one-in-twenty-five poor children attending some form of schooling.

With this new social challenge, a tremendous amount of information was dispensed to people vis-à-vis the church pulpit on a variety of subjects—from biblical truths to ethics to social norms to nationalistic ideals. Aside from the minority presence of the remaining non-conformists in England, the Anglican Church controlled much of the information and social services dispensed in English society. Puritanism, which had been so strong a century earlier, had migrated across the Atlantic to the former colonies in America, and Englanders were left with a rigid, impersonal, coldly-institutional, Christian community from which to receive both spiritual and physical aid.

---

1. Halliday, *England*, 158.

Whereas earlier in England the striving for a personal, biblical faith was encouraged (and mandated in some circles), eighteenth-century parishioners found a more hierarchical church scene wherein the rich, social elite enjoyed the fruits and focus of most religious offerings. Deism, a qualifiedly detached form of spiritual belief, was the stylish norm; personal zeal or enthusiasm was frowned upon; but commoners found themselves wanting and needing more from church leaders. As Curtis notes, "In this world of little hope and few options, John Wesley appeared on the scene"[2]—a scene that he would challenge, spiritually and ethically.

Wesley's Upbringing

Although Wesley's grandparents were non-conformist Puritans, Wesley's memoir must begin with a description of his parents, Samuel and Susanna. "Samuel, John's father, was an [Oxford] scholar, for many years at work on a monumental scholarly work on the Book of Job. A stern, relentless [Anglican] preacher . . ."[3] Still, his father is often portrayed as a strong willed (and sometimes less than wise) father, rector, and scholar who had trouble managing both money and politics. Wesley's mother is frequently presented as a kind-though-serious woman who often had to raise her children by herself in many ways—"Susanna Wesley's regime at the parsonage was very strict even by eighteenth century standards. She bore many children—John was the fourteenth—but Susanna Wesley knew precisely what to do with them. She broke her children's wills early so that their young minds could be formed in a wholly Christian fashion."[4]

Considering his parental influences, it becomes fathomable why Wesley interpreted life and the Christian walk as he did. The dynamic yet resolute spirit of his father is easily seen manifesting

---

2. Curtis, "Revival and Revolution," 8.
3. Curtis, "John Wesley and Women," 8.
4. Curtis, "John Wesley and Women," 26.

itself alongside of the disciplined yet loving spirit of his mother. Collins says of them,

> These two earnest and sincere people, these strong personalities, together provided an atmosphere in the Epworth Rectory that would instill an uncanny seriousness in moral and spiritual affairs in many of their children with the good result that all three of their sons . . . would eventually become priests of the Church of England.[5]

Wesley appears to have synthesized these qualities in his own personal ethos and ministry—sending him on a personal quest for a pure and intense relationship with God. The integration of his personality and upbringing with his faith was a long process involving much conflict, contemplation, courage, and change.

It is important to note that as a young boy (besides growing up under the strong emotional influence of his parents) Wesley's spiritual path was also affected by a devastating fire that took the Epworth Rectory (and nearly his life) in 1709.[6] Young Wesley's escape bordered on the miraculous, and so it is no wonder that his parents began to believe and wonder if God had a special work for Wesley to do. As Collins states, "The fire revealed to John Wesley not only God's superintending providence, but all that the Lord had perhaps a special plan, a noble purpose, for his life."[7] From then on, Wesley " . . . never doubted God's providential hand upon his life."[8] He came to feel that he had a direct calling from God—although this calling was often bittersweet and mysterious, at times.

From Boy to Young Scholar

With urging from his parents, Wesley's spiritual journey took him from home in Epworth, Lincolnshire to Oxford College where he would become ordained as an Anglican priest, later to travel to

---

5. Collins, *A Real Christian*, 20.
6. Gonzalez, *The Story of Christianity*, 265.
7. Collins, *A Real Christian*, 14.
8. Shelley, *Church History in Plain Language*, 333.

Georgia in America as a missionary to the colonists and indigenous Indians.[9]

During this early formational period Wesley's sense of spiritual conscience grew and changed in various ways. For one, he came to understand that a full understanding and personal application of biblical wisdom was unattainable without clear intentions and concerted discipline; however, "The early Wesley was dissatisfied not only with his own Christian experience, but with that of others as well."[10]

To improve upon his spiritual situation, at Oxford, John Wesley joined a spiritual club (and eventually led it in 1729) begun by his own brother, Charles, which was called, ostensibly, "The Holy Club" (among other nicknames). The group followed a "rigid religious regimen, which later included early rising, Bible study, and prison ministry."[11] Additionally, according to Wesley's second Oxford journal, each day, members of the club would ruminate on questions such as "Did the Bible live in me today? When did I last speak to someone else of my faith? Do I insist upon doing something about which my conscience is uneasy? Am I defeated in any part of my life? Is Christ real to me?"[12]

The main goal of the Holy Club was to increase spiritual vitality through thoughtful consideration of God's word and its application in the loathsome workhouses and prisons shunned by other Anglican ministers. With his father part of the vaulted high church, this was the first time that John and Charles Wesley experienced such intense, in-the-trenches, face-to-face time with commoners, and John came to appreciate more of their spiritual needs and even their sincere gifts. Notable future ministerial celebrities of this envied club included John Gambold, John Clayton, James Hervey, Benjamin Ignham, and even the famed George Whitefield.

By the time he was ordained in 1725 and received his Master of Arts degree in 1727, Wesley embarked on a mission to help those

9. Gonzalez, *The Story of Christianity*, 266.
10. Collins, *A Real Christian*, 24.
11. Townsend, "The Forgotten Wesley," 7.
12. Archive.org, "Preface."

around him (and himself) to become better, authentic Christians. In his journal, Wesley writes, "I began to see that true Religion was seated in the heart, and that God's law extended to all our thoughts as well as words and actions."[13] He sought this through advocating spiritual discipline, cultivation, and application. He would eventually return to England where his methodology, once matured, would influence England, dramatically.

First Love

Being a young man, Wesley, of course, had to deal with the typical domestic questions in life. Would he get married? Where would he pastor? Curtis records, "Throughout his life John Wesley was naturally attracted to women, and he attracted a wide range of women to him. Although he was disappointed in love and more so in his marriage, nevertheless, for spiritual comradeship, Wesley especially cherished contact with faithful women."[14] Wesley's seriousness about women and their courting began in college, whereat he socialized and rubbed elbows with professorial and ministerial families and friends, many of which who had daughters of marrying age, such as the Granville and Kirkham sisters.

In particular, at Oxford, Wesley felt strong emotions for one Sally Kirkham, the daughter of Reverend Lionel Kirkham (the Rector of Stanton), and certainly would have married her, but despite his fondness and love for her, he never proposed matrimony and she ended up marrying a schoolteacher—the Reverend John Chapone in 1725. Sally's decision might have been quite intuitive because Wesley often spoke that "God must not only be his highest love, but also, in a real sense, his only love."[15] This extreme attitude would create not only self-conflict, but also frequently pit him against family, friends, and adversaries alike throughout his life. With Sally eventually married to another, and with his father

---

13. Curtis, "John Wesley and Women," 30.
14. Ibid., 25.
15. Collins, *A Real Christian*, 35.

encouraging him to follow his footsteps at the Rectory, Wesley made a decision that would dramatically change his life.

Ministerial Awakenings

Despite the unexpected death of their father in 1735, John and Charles prayerfully decided to utilize their education and ministerial skills as missionaries to the Americas (also inspiring George Whitefield and Thomas Coke to do so, subsequently). As Noll states, "During the second century of colonization, events in America began to shape the character of Christian life and faith more decisively."[16] Namely, the (first) Great Awakening (1730–1740), a revivalist movement started in New England, was a watershed moment for American churches tired of religious social malaise and ready to return to the original passion and purity of their Calvinist roots. Through the powerful preaching of men such as Jonathan Edwards, Theo Frelinghuysen, and George Whitefield, the three main concepts of renewed spirituality (terror of the law to sinners, the unmerited grace of God, and new birth in Jesus Christ) swept southward, captivating numerous consciences and congregations for God.

The American colonies were, from their establishment, a mixed bag of religious offerings—Puritan, Quaker, Anglican, and Catholic. The Virginia colony was founded during the high point of Puritanism in England; however, the first expeditions' main goals were to set up the Church of England in the region. The New England colonies (Connecticut, Massachusetts) were founded with Puritanism in mind; Maryland was to be Catholic; Pennsylvania was governed by Quaker William Penn (although with much religious freedom in Penn's governmental charter); however, the founding of some colonies was based more on economic opportunity and religious freedoms than religious hegemony such as the colonies of New York, New Jersey, Delaware, Rhode Island, and Georgia.

16. Noll, *A History of Christianity*, 83.

Mission to America

Georgia was the last English colony to be named for an English monarch (King George II). With lands taken from South Carolina territory, it was set up mainly to be a buffer zone between Britain's colonies and Spanish Florida. Colonization was highly restricted, at first: no one could own more than five hundred acres, women could not own farms, colonists could not sell land to each other, slavery was banned, and anyone willing to work there was allowed (including English prisoners).

Religiously, Georgia was both individualistic and undefined. Nichols writes, "There was not an established church from Georgia's founding in 1732 until 1758, at which time the Church of England became the 'official' religion of the colony until the Revolution. But even then, the legal establishment in Georgia was, in practice, a weak (or 'soft') establishment with little real ecclesiastical presence."[17] Such a golden evangelistic opportunity was too good to pass for many ministers and missionaries in England. Wesley hoped that this assignment would not only allow him to preach to sinners and heathens, but to also work on his own spiritual state and aid him in becoming more holy.

As Vickers explains,

> Methodism itself was essentially a missionary movement. Mission was its raison d'être. Indeed, the missionary perspective and commitment were there from the outset in John Wesley's own background and experience. There was a missionary emphasis in his family, passed on to him through his mother, and it was a natural expression of this that led the Wesley brothers to offer for Georgia in 1735.[18]

So, with their mother's approval, in 1735, Wesley left England with his brother, Charles, as well as a number of the Moravian Brethren for the Georgia colony. This would prove to be a pivotal trip for Wesley, as Durnbaugh notes, "The connection of John

17. Nichols, "Religious Liberty in the Thirteenth Colony," 1696.
18. Vickers, "One-man Band," 135.

Wesley (1703–1791) and Pietism is both personal and doctrinal. Wesley was profoundly influenced by the Moravians, on the way to his brief mission effort in Georgia, while in Georgia, and upon his return in disgrace to England."[19]

The Moravians, like other branches of Pietism (Halle, Reformed, Radical), sought to revive the church through personal spiritual renewal, to "breathe new life into dead churches" and spiritually-dead people, presumably. To accomplish this, they emphasized personal, pragmatic holiness along with authentic, experiential faith. Moreover, they embraced scripture as the chief means of renewal, acted kindly and properly in controversial matters, utilized the priesthood of all believers, and ensured their sermons were both evangelistic and focused on the love of God for all humanity.

As Curtis concludes,

> Pietists were basically interested in the religious renewal of the individual, belief in the Bible as the unfailing guide to faith and life, a complete commitment to Christ which must be evident in the Christian's life, the need for Christian nurture through the faithful use of appropriate devotional aids, including sermons and hymns, and finally a concern to apply the love of Christ so as to alleviate the social and cultural ills of the day.[20]

Crossing the Atlantic in the eighteenth century was no easy or secure voyage—quite the opposite. Not surprisingly, during Wesley's fateful trip, the ship encountered several violent storms that threatened to tear the ship apart and send him to his end. Wesley was terribly afraid, but was also astounded at the peace and confidence his Moravian co-travelers exhibited in the midst of the chaos around them. Whereas his faith seemed too little to bolster his spirits, "As the sea broke over the deck of the vessel, splitting the mainsail in pieces, the Moravians calmly sang their psalms to

---

19. Durnbaugh, "The Flowering of Pietism," 25.
20. Curtis, "What is Pietism?" 3.

God."²¹ With great envy, Wesley observed their strength of faith and resolved to have it himself, some day.

In the Georgia colony, with renewed zeal, Wesley utilized an almost ascetic lifestyle, attempting to deny his flesh for the Lord. Complicating matters, he not only required this standard of himself, but also attempted to force it upon all in his parish, including his newest love interest—Sophy Hopkey, which would eventually catapult him back to England in failure. Wesley felt a strong romantic attraction for the younger Sophy, a relative of the chief magistrate of Savannah, but "Wesley was so mixed up emotionally and spiritually that he didn't know his own mind."²²

He attempted through various means to control his emotions, which eventually led her to elope with another man. Perhaps partly because of his jealousy or bitterness, or perhaps because of a true burden to ensure purity of faith, Wesley soon thereafter "barred her from Holy Communion, and her incensed husband sued John for defaming Sophy's character."²³ Politically, all this accomplished was Wesley receiving a one-way ticket back to England, "sadly discredited and painfully uncertain of his faith and future."²⁴

On his voyage home, Wesley re-evaluated his ministerial plans and purposes in the colonies, and came to several important conclusions. Self-admittedly, while in Georgia, he suffered from disbelief, pride, irrecollection, levity, and luxuriancy of spirit.²⁵ In other words, instead of focusing his ministry in the service of God, he was "of two minds and two wills."²⁶ He believed that he had failed because of his humanity, his works-righteousness reigning rather than a simple, sincere love of God and others.

---

21. Shelley, 331.
22. Ibid., 335.
23. Ibid., 335.
24. Ibid., 335.
25. Outler, "An Early Self-Analysis," 41.
26. Collins, *A Real Christian*, 53.

Reflection and Repentance

From this point on, with greater insight and humility, Wesley began to define and hone his understanding of the faith—both in doctrine and practice. "With a conviction that he must not simply seek personal holiness, but spread a message of salvation as far as he could, Wesley embarked on a lifetime's mission throughout the British Isles."[27] He wanted people to know that " . . . grace must become actual, not simply possible; grace must be realized, not simply imagined,"[28] that a Christian is one "[W]ho so believes in Christ as that sin hath no more dominion over him,"[29] and that "a justified person is freed from the guilt of sin, a regenerated one from its power, and the entirely sanctified from its being."[30] Wesley began to move towards Christian Perfection as an attainable ideal.

During this period, Wesley also began preaching provocative views alongside Calvinist George Whitefield, whom Noll calls "[T]he best-known Protestant in the whole world during the eighteenth century,"[31] in a series of outdoor revivals. Wesley and Whitefield's success came much to the disfavor and disapproval of the Anglican Church (although Wesley always held that his work was meant to supplement and not replace the ministry of the Church of England) who found their enthusiasm distasteful and destruction to proper social structure—"[T]hey were called enthusiasts because they preached the Holy Spirit. The majority of people hungered for their appeal to non-rational impulses, but ministers of the Anglican Church, who hated enthusiasm, shut their doors to this renewed appeal to deep spiritual reserves."[32]

Wesley struggled to maintain contacts within the Anglican Church, going as far as to not have his services or meetings at the same time as the regular Anglican services. Shelley writes, "Wesley

---

27. MacCulloch, *Christianity*, 750.
28. Collins, *John Wesley*, 81.
29. Baker, "Letters," 575.
30. Collins, *John Wesley*, 96.
31. Noll, *A History of Christianity*, 91.
32. Curtis, "John Wesley and Women," 27.

resisted all pressures from his own followers and all charges from Anglican bishops that he separate from the Church of England."[33] Instead, he worked to create and sustain productive centers of support to Christianity in England (and later America). Doctrinally and pragmatically, though, Wesley migrated more and more away from the standard, mandated (and stagnant) church practices in English society until he was barred from speaking at Oxford University and even became estranged from his revivalist mentor and comrade, Whitefield, over doctrinal matters.[34]

Although they had been friends and ministerial partners for many years, the two revivalists came into conflict over the notions of predestination and grace. Walsh writes,

> The Wesleys were unshakable "Arminians" who denied predestination, yet the revival drew zealous recruits from areas in which Puritan Calvinism was much alive. At first, Whitefield was no predestinarian, but by the time he sailed to America in the summer of 1739, he was reading Calvinist books. Contact with fervent American Calvinists filled out his knowledge.[35]

Still, the two had a very respectful and kind relationship with each other after they parted ways in 1740 because, as Walsh concludes, "Far more united the antagonists than ever separated them."[36]

Wesley's Methodology

With less contemporary constraints, Wesley started to utilize the laity in his ministry, adding to the disdain of the Anglican Church, which criticized the dangerous lack of education of many of Wesley's appointed lay preachers. In the meantime, Wesley, who "... relished organizing people,"[37] set out to help his followers

---

33. Shelley, 339–340.
34. Gonzalez, *The Story of Christianity*, 268.
35. Walsh, 35–36.
36. Ibid., 36.
37. MacCulloch, *Christianity*, 750.

to higher holiness through the United Societies, whose purpose was to "Do no harm and avoid evil of all sorts. Do good of every possible sort, and insofar as possible to all people. Observe the ordinances of God, including public worship, the ministry of the Word read from Scripture"[38] and the Methodist class, whose main purpose was "chiefly one of discipline."[39]

The first was a broad umbrella covering all members; the latter was more specifically involved in the sharpening and refining of Methodist brothers and sisters in Christ. More specifically, Wesley developed several different support groups to aid in Christian spiritual and behavioral transformations. There was "The Society" group, which utilized lay leaders and assistants in the education of its members; there was "The Class Meeting," which was not voluntary but required and experiential; there was "The Band," which was homogeneous in gender and confessional; there was "The Select Society," which, although democratic, focused on the needs and training of leaders in the Methodist Movement; finally, there was "The Penitent Society," whose main focus was mainstreaming others into the faith and movement.

Although he never called it such, Wesley's approach to cultivating personal Christian spiritual growth came to be called,

> the Wesleyan Quadrilateral, and included scripture, tradition, reason, and experience. Scripture is considered the primary source and standard for Christian doctrine. Tradition is experience and the witness of development and growth of the faith through the past centuries and in many nations and cultures. Experience is the individual's understanding and appropriating of the faith in the light of his or her own life. Through reason the individual Christian brings to bear on the Christian faith discerning and cogent thought.[40]

Wesley may not have invented these ideas, but he certainly combined them, successfully.

38. Corbett-Hemeyer, *Religion in America*, 56.
39. Collins, *A Real Christian*, 81.
40. UMC.org, "Wesleyan Quadrilateral."

Wesley and Education

One area that Wesley also ventured into concerned public education. Body suggests that Wesley saw the state of teaching in England to be woefully lacking because, "not only were the subjects ill chosen but the method of attack was often ignorantly planned."[41] Wesley saw many subjects being neglected with thinking and learning being a low priority to the detriment of the student. Adding to this, Wesley believed most schools were not geographically well placed, cutting off new scholars and enabling inappropriate students to enroll.

At Kingswood School, which Wesley founded (along with other charity schools), his philosophy utilized and idealized the educational methods of famous teachers like Plato, Locke, Milton, Rousseau, Edgeworth, and also the Moravians, whose influence in Wesley's life cannot be overstated. Wesley utilized the educational theories of these "greats" to build and maintain several schools that provided "something better than the regular education of the eighteenth century."[42] Therefore, for Wesley, the ultimate goal of education was "that it should be a means to the great end of saving the souls of the children."[43] In this regard, he did not attempt to separate academics from religion.

In fact, he suggested that they were inseparable—contrary to the practice and thought of his time. Towns states, "He did not believe in the religious education merely because he was a minister, he definitely believed that the two ideas (religion and education) were mutually dependent and that in no uncertain manner, the righteous prospered as the green bay tree mentally while the unrighteous sowed the wind of ungodliness and reaped a whirlwind of perpetual ignorance."[44]

Not without some controversy, Wesley "built up his educational scheme of sound religious training combined with perfect

41. Body, 47.
42. Ibid., 33.
43. Ibid., 74.
44. Towns, 321.

control of the children."[45] Discipline was the key and his students were allowed little free time to get in trouble. They were constantly under supervision and were provided with a rigorous daily schedule consisting of prayer, school, exercise, gardening, work, more prayer, and worship. Their diet was sufficient but not opulent. Wesley permitted no play days and insisted the children spend all of their time at the school as home life tended to corrupt their attitudes and behaviors. Masters and other workers were constantly being hired and fired as they came into conflict with Wesley's educational system. Wesley often had to battle with his employees to maintain standards. He also struggled to find funding for his Spartan schools.

Matrimonial Strife

As the Methodist movement expanded, though, Wesley naturally encountered more criticism and controversy in his ministerial and personal life. Never lacking drama on the romantic front, Wesley found himself in matrimonial chaos, nearly marrying one woman (Grace Murray) until his brother, in a roundabout attempt to help John find someone "Better," convinced Grace to dissolve her engagement to John and to marry another suitor. Not surprisingly, Wesley was heartbroken (if not also enraged), and so, without even conferring with his brother, he wed Mary ("Molly") Vazeille, the wife of a merchant killed at sea.

Perhaps John hoped to channel his anger positively into the noble, biblical rescue of a needy widow, but Curtis suggests it to be, "one of the worst mistakes of his life."[46] To say the two were incompatible, both in personality and life-goals, would be hyperbolic understatement of the greatest measure. In fact, Wesley's ministerial duties and aspirations often kept him away from his new wife, and she chided the evangelist, condemned his choices, calling him callous, authoritarian, and self-righteous (if not self-absorbed). She

---

45. Body, 52.
46. Curtis, "John Wesley and Women," 27.

also accused him of adultery because of his frequent affectionate letters that he would send to other women of faith that he admired and supported in their search for Christian Perfection.

As Busenitz states,

> Due to her husband's constant travels, Molly felt increasingly neglected. She grew jealous of her husband's time since he was often away. And she became suspicious of the many friendly relationships he maintained with various women who were part of the Methodist movement. Wesley for his part did little to assuage her fears. Consequently, their marriage was a rocky one.[47]

Ironically, despite appearances that seemed to suggest him being a distant, neglectful, and insensitive husband to Molly, several of his peers recorded physical abuse from Molly on Wesley. They separated in 1751, and she returned to his side a few times before her death at his heartfelt bequest. Confirming their incompatibility, she would soon depart again, unhappy and unwilling to accept the personal foibles and habits that made Wesley such a formidable evangelist.

They never divorced, but it is clear both considered their marriage to be a colossal mistake. Unfortunately, not much is known, conclusively—especially since Wesley only recorded one entry about her and their tumultuous relationship in his journal.[48] In it, he wrote, "Finally, she left for good . . . I did not forsake her, I did not dismiss her, I will not recall her."[49] Yet, despite his marital troubles, Curtis notes, "For Wesley, women had equal stature to men in God's eyes. He used women in his work, and he elaborated

---

47. Busenitz, "John Wesley's Failed Marriage."

48. During Wesley's journey toward sanctification, he kept a journal, which was not unusual for the era. The unique aspects of his journal was more in its spiritual depth and discussion, and in its volume of information. In Wesley's journal, readers can find information on the work of God in his life as well as those around him, they can find advice and commentary on preaching methodology, and find a personal history on the founder of the Methodist Movement.

49. CCEL.org, *The Journal of the Rev. John Wesley*.

on the special service of women who died doing good for the poor and for prisoners."[50]

Wesley and Division

Compounding this tension, Wesley had other forces to contend with in life—officially defining what it meant to be a Methodist, defending himself from Protestant attacks against his ministry, and working out the logistics of establishing the Methodist movement and workers in America. This occasionally pitted him against the establishment and other jealous or disagreeable preachers, who often acted in extremist or half-hearted fashion toward Wesley. Furthermore, there was a faction of new Methodists who wanted to split away from the Church of England, which Wesley disagreed with, whole-heartedly. Anglicans found Wesley's practices undesirable and "[It] was maintained by some clergy, for instance, that Methodism with its significant and ever growing infrastructure was causing a division, a schism, in the church."[51]

These schisms were not limited to the Church of England, alone. According to Pediar, "Generally, speaking, the Calvinist tradition has seen sovereignty through the model of a ruling monarch, whereas Wesley conceived of sovereignty primary through the model of a loving parent."[52] Additionally, Collins remarks that Wesley's insistence that true faith consists of an obedient heart "... led Calvinists to conclude that Wesley was, in effect, teaching salvation by works."[53]

Wesley, of course, completely disputed this claim, which is evident in his *A Plain Account of Christian Perfection*, especially in chapter eleven, where he references the influence of grace in the life of the believer eleven times, and succinctly stating, "If we were not utterly impotent, our good works would be our own property;

50. Curtis, "John Wesley and Women," 27.
51. Collins, *A Real Christian*, 98.
52. Pedlar, "John Wesley on Predestination."
53. Collins, *A Real Christian*, 131.

whereas now they belong wholly to God, because they proceed from Him and His grace: while raising our works, and making them all divine, He honours Himself in us through them."[54]

Additionally, in *How To Pray: The Best of John Wesley on Prayer*, he states, "I continue to dream and pray about a revival of holiness in our day that moves forth in mission and creates authentic community in which each person can be unleashed through the empowerment of the Spirit to fulfill God's creational intentions."[55] In Wesley's mind, any perfection and predestination began and continued by the grace and efforts of the Holy Spirit, and not humanity.

Of course, writing challenging treatises such as *The Question, What is an Arminian? Answered by a Lover of Free Grace* (1765), did not help his reputation with many ardent Calvinists. As Wood notes, "Taking his cue from the Dutch theologian Jacob Arminius (1560–1609), Wesley contended that each human being possessed the moral agency to accept or reject Christ's offer of redemption."[56] The Calvinists found Wesley's ideas to be quite troubling, and they considered his interpretation of Christianity to be unsound, doctrinally, if not downright heretical.

Wesley and the American Revolutionary War

Finally, another schism involving Wesley revolved around the American colonies that wished to separate from the British Empire. Many American ministers

> considered independence from England a just, Godly cause for liberty, especially considering the economic and social abuses of King George III in American colonial lands. The Boston Massacre (March 5, 1770) and the deaths of five colonists at the hands of British soldiers during that deadly event provoked many pro-Revolution,

---

54. Wesley, *A Plain Account of Christian Perfection*, 111.
55. Wesley, *How to Pray*.
56. Wood, "That They May Be Free Indeed," 231.

anti-English sermons from colonial pulpits, which would continue throughout the war.[57]

As a loyal British subject, Wesley thought the colonists were haughty in their demands, unloving, and disrespectful in their attitudes toward their paternal country.

He writes in *A Calm Address to the American Colonies*,

> Have pity upon your mother country! Have pity upon your own! Have pity upon yourselves, upon your children, and upon all that are near and dear to you! Let us not bite and devour one another, lest we be consumed one of another! O let us follow after peace! Let us put away our sins; the real ground of all our calamities; which never will or can be thoroughly removed, till we fear God and honour the king![58]

For Wesley, being a full-hearted Christian meant loving one's neighbors, unconditionally—even across the great Atlantic—and with a servant's heart. He perceived the rebellious colonists doing neither, and let them know, directly.

Not surprisingly, many Americans challenged Wesley's acquiescent ideas, pointing to the righteous rebellion of Jesus and the Apostles in the face of Imperial corruption and exploitation. Like their Puritan ancestors, they hoped "of achieving the corporate holiness in church and community that seemed unattainable in old England."[59] Wesley's vocal objections to the American revolutionaries added yet another facet of factionalism to deal with later in his life as he worked to establish and ordain ministers in the former colonies.

It is surprising that Wesley did not encounter more persecution and controversy than he did in his later years (especially considering the culture and social senses originated in him by his parents). Still, Wesley was famous, worldwide, for having a loving heart for God and those in need. Furthermore, he was opinionated,

---

57. Knox, "John Lathrop," 1319.
58. Consource.org, "A Calm Address to the American Colonies."
59. Packer, "Theology on Fire," 32.

but he was also an intelligent man of convictions who did not compromise on divine truth that directed his paths, warmed his heart, and provided a resolute goal. Thus, it is no surprise that his relationship with the Anglican Church began to unravel in his later years.

First, after the American Revolutionary War, despite Wesley's intense evangelical desires to place the reins of American Christianity in capable American clergy hands, "The bishop of London, who supposedly still had jurisdiction over the former colonies, refused to ordain personnel for the United States."[60] Second, as Gonzalez writes,

> According to English law, non-Anglican services and church buildings were to be allowed, but they must be officially registered as such. This put the Methodist in a difficult situation, for the Church of England did not acknowledge their meetings and buildings. If they registered, this would be a tacit declaration that they were not Anglicans. If they did not, they would be breaking the law.[61]

Methodism Stands Alone

Pushing back against the politicization of religion between the two countries, Wesley relied upon ancient church history to justify the ordination of two lay ministers in America (Richard Whatcost and Thomas Vasey) and others in Scotland. Embracing an early patristic tradition that equated presbyters and elders with the bishopric, which he felt implied that ordained ministers such as himself could anoint and appoint the willing and able. Shelley calls this, "An important breach in Anglican policy."[62]

Pushing his philosophy even further, he later named Anglican priests Thomas Coke and Francis Asbury as co-superintendents

---

60. Gonzalez, *The Story of Christianity*, 272.
61. Ibid., 271–272.
62. Shelley, 340.

in America. As Curtis records, "Joining the Methodists in 1771, [Coke] rose quickly under Wesley to become president of the Irish conference in 1782 and joint superintendent with Francis Asbury of the Methodist Church of America in 1794."[63] This move shocked and vexed the Church of England, who considered the whole affair tantamount to organizational mutiny (although in defense, Wesley said that he was only trying to meet the needs of people unmet by the Church of England in America and Britain).

Despite Wesley's appointment of the two Methodist leaders in America, he became displeased with Asbury, particularly, because Wesley assumed his commission would be taken, authoritatively; however, "Instead of asserting his right to govern by virtue of Wesley's decree, Asbury subjected himself to a vote of confirmation by the preachers at the conference."[64] Thereafter, American Methodists operated more independently, even "increasingly hostile"[65] toward their English founder than before the American Revolution.

With little other choice, Wesley advised his ministers to register, legally severing his/their relationship with the Anglican Church (although to his death Wesley never admitted the official creation of the Methodist Church). The Methodist movement continued to develop and modify to English and American culture (especially considering the Industrial Revolution underway in England and the expansion into new territories in the United States) and "filled a need and found most of its members."[66] However, as America's diversity was increasing year by year, so did Methodism also begin to adapt and develop into various expressions under the Methodist "umbrella."

---

63. Curtis, "A Gallery of Family," 12.
64. Wood, 236.
65. Ibid., 237.
66. Gonzalez, *The Story of Christianity*, 273.

Wesley, the Elder

As Wesley moved into his senior years, he often recorded how pleased he was with his on-going strength and vitality, which allowed him to continue his ministry and evangelism. In his journal, he writes, "This day I entered the sixty-ninth year of my age. I am still a wonder to myself. My voice and strength are the same as at nine and twenty. This also hath God wrought."[67] Some years later, he added in his journal, "The chief means are: (1) My constantly rising at four, for about fifty years. (2) My generally preaching at five in the morning, one of the most healthy exercises in the world. (3) My never travelling less, by sea or land, than four thousand five hundred miles in a year."[68] However, being a mere mortal, Wesley finally succumbed to the great equalizer (death), writing one year before his passing,

> But last August, I found almost a sudden change. My eyes were so dim that no glasses would help me. My strength likewise now quite forsook me and probably will not return in this world. But I feel no pain from head to foot, only it seems nature is exhausted and, humanly speaking, will sink more and more, till 'The wear springs of life stand still at last.'[69]

Thus, Wesley died on March 2, 1790, surrounded by friends, with his final message of encouragement—"The best of all is, God is with us."[70]

Soon thereafter, the English Methodists separated from the Church of England just as their American brothers had done, earlier, but the movement that Wesley had begun to supplement church life had quickly become the foundation of a new and efficacious Christian culture. Shelley writes, "Wesley's impact and the revival he represents carried far beyond the Methodist Church. It renewed the religious life of England and her colonies. It elevated

---

67. CCEL.org, "The Earl of Desmond's Castle."
68. CCEL.org, "Wesley's Terrible Ride."
69. CCEL.org, "The Last Year of the Journal."
70. Hurst, 298.

the life of the poor. It stimulated overseas missions and the social concerns of evangelicals in the nineteenth and the twentieth centuries."[71]

Wesley's Legacy

It would not be an overstatement to say that John Wesley was a well-versed man of God, both in reading and writing. Still, his life was more than just one of scholarship and pondering. Wesley was also a man of productive evangelical action until his last days, traveling over 250,000 miles on horseback and delivering more than 40,000 sermons, worldwide. Roger Green states, "He also published selections of his sermons and wrote voluminously. His use of lay preachers and small 'societies' spread the movement to some 120,000 followers by the time of his death."[72]

As Olsen notes, "Without debate, Wesley himself held to the supreme authority of Scripture over every other source and norm for Christian preaching and living. On the other hand, he included reason, tradition and experience as essential interpretive tools for doing theology."[73] Gonzalez states, "John Wesley, the founder of Methodism, combined the religious zeal of the Moravians with the social activism that had long characterized the Reformed tradition."[74] George Whitefield, himself, wrote of his former associate, "My brother Wesley acted wisely—the souls that were awakened under his ministry he joined in societies, and thus preserved the fruits of his labor. This I neglected, and my people are a rope of sand."[75]

One of the biggest regrets of the dying is not pursuing one's dream or calling in life.[76] For himself and others, Wesley

71. Shelley, 340.
72. Green, "1738 John & Charles Wesley Experience Conversions."
73. Olsen, 513.
74. Gonzalez, *The Story of Christianity*, 265.
75. Wesley Center Online, "Chapter XIII—In Conference with the Preachers."
76. Steiner, "Top Five Regrets of the Dying."

frequently vocalized his hopes that all believers, in reaching their own "Golden Years," could look back and see as long, as priceless of a legacy of sanctification and sincere love as he accomplished despite his personal faults and life challenges—if not in teaching and preaching to people about God, at least in modeling and striving for holiness of heart and mind, which was never more evident than in Wesley's fifty-two sermons.

TIMELINE

1703	Birth of John Wesley
1707	Birth of Charles Wesley
1709	Rescued from Epworth Rectory fire
1720	Admitted to Oxford College
1725	Ordained deacon
1726	Elected fellow of Lincoln College, Oxford
1728	Ordained priest in the Anglican Church
1728	Becomes leader of Oxford Club
1735	Death of Samuel Wesley, Wesley's father
1735	John and Charles Wesley sail for Georgia
1738	Wesley's conversion on Aldersgate Street
1739	Wesley's first open-air sermon
1740	Wesley and the Moravians part ways
1741	First time preaching in South Wales
1742	Death of Susanna Wesley, Wesley's mother
1742	Wesleys found orphanage & Sunday School
1744	First Methodist conference
1746	Founds dispensary for the poor
1747	First time preaching in Ireland
1751	First time preaching in Scotland
1751	Wesley marries Mary Vazeille
1755	Wesley separates from his wife
1768	Methodist Chapel opens in New York
1775	Wesley writes "A Calm Address"
1781	Death of Wesley's wife, Mary
1784	Ordination of Thomas Coke/Francis Asbury
1788	Death of Charles Wesley
1791	Death of John Wesley

3

Annotated Sermon Summaries

Sermon 1: "Salvation By Faith"

Key Bible Verse(s): "For by grace are ye saved through faith; and that not of yourselves: it is the gift of God" (Ephesians 2:8).

Summary: Salvation and faith are a gift of God that should be exercised and apparent from the manifest heart of the Christian.

Location & Date: St. Mary's, Oxford; June 11, 1738

Main Themes: Grace, Faith, and Salvation

Key Quotations and Passages:

- "He that is, by faith, born of God sinneth not (1.) by any habitual sin; for all habitual sin is sin reigning ... Nor (2.) by any wilful sin ... Nor (3.) By any sinful desire ... Nor (4.) Doth he sin by infirmities."
- "For all our works, all our righteousness, which were before our believing, merited nothing of God but condemnation; so far were they from deserving faith, which therefore, whenever given, is not of works. Neither is salvation of the works we do when we believe, for it is then God that worketh in us:

and, therefore, that he giveth us a reward for what he himself worketh, only commendeth the riches of his mercy, but leaveth us nothing whereof to glory."

Sermon 2: "The Almost Christian"

Key Bible Verse(s): "Then Agrippa said unto Paul, almost thou persuadest me to be a Christian" (Acts 26:28).

Summary: The key to life is love of God and humanity, and obedience to God.

Location & Date: St. Mary's, Oxford; June 25, 1741

Main Themes: Half-Christian, True Christianity, and Faith

Key Quotations and Passages:

- "[T]he common heathens allowed, that some regard was to be paid to truth, as well as to justice."
- "[T]here was a sort of love and assistance which they expected one from another."
- "It is a sure trust and confidence which a man hath in God, that, by the merits of Christ, his sins are forgiven, and he reconciled to the favour of God; whereof doth follow a loving heart, to obey his commandments."

Sermon 3: "Awake, Thou That Sleepest"

Key Bible Verse(s): "Wherefore he saith, awake thou that sleepest, and arise from the dead, and Christ shall give thee light" (Ephesians 5:14).

Summary: Wesley's sermon is a call for his parishioners to reality, to repentance, and to living a full life.

Location & Date: University of Oxford; April 4, 1742

Main Themes: Asleep, Darkness, Complacency, and Enlightenment

Key Quotations and Passages:

- "By one who sleeps, we are, therefore, to understand (and would to God we might all understand it!) a sinner satisfied in his sins; contented to remain in his fallen state, to live and die without the image of God; one who is ignorant both of his disease, and of the only remedy for it; one who never was warned, or never regarded the warning voice of God."
- "[H]e wants nothing of godliness, but the power; nothing of religion, but the spirit; nothing of Christianity, but the truth and the life."
- "[D]o not ye harden your hearts, and resist the Holy Ghost, who even now is come to convince you of sin."
- "God is light, and will give himself to every awakened sinner that waiteth for him; and thou shalt then be a temple of the living God."

Sermon 4: "Scriptural Christianity"

Key Bible Verse(s): "And when they had prayed, the place was shaken where they were assembled together; and they were all filled with the Holy Ghost, and they spake the word of God with boldness" (Acts 4:31).

Summary: In this sermon, Wesley gives evidences for what it meant to be a Christian in the New Testament, the struggles of pure faith in the early church years, and the state of Christianity in his era.

Location & Date: St. Mary's, Oxford; August 24, 1744

Main Themes: Pentecost, Spiritual Cultivation, and Christian Application

Key Quotations and Passages:

- "[T]he mind which was in Christ, those holy fruits of the Spirit . . . to endue them with faith (perhaps it might be rendered, fidelity), with meekness and temperance; to enable them to crucify the flesh, with its affections and lusts, its passions and desires; and in consequence of that inward change, to fulfill all outward righteousness."

- "Do ye, brethren, abound in the fruits of the Spirit, in lowliness of mind, in self-denial and mortification, in seriousness and composure of spirit, in patience, meekness, sobriety, temperance; and in unwearied, restless endeavours to do good in every kind unto all men, to relieve their outward wants, and to bring their souls to the true knowledge and love of God?"

Sermon 5: "Justification By Faith"

Key Bible Verse(s): "But to him that worketh not, but believeth on him that justifieth the ungodly, his faith is counted for righteousness" (Romans 4:5).

Summary: In his message, Wesley explains what justification is, who is justified, and who reaps its benefits.

Main Themes: Justification, Law, Faith, and Sin

Key Quotations and Passages:

- "This, therefore, is the general ground of the whole doctrine of justification. By the sin of the first Adam . . . likewise the representative, of us all, we all fell short of the favour of God; we all became children of wrath . . . Even so, by the sacrifice for sin made by the Second Adam, as the Representative of us all, God is so far reconciled to all the world, that he hath given them a new covenant."

- "God justifieth not the godly, but the ungodly; not those that are holy already, but the unholy."

- "Faith, therefore, is the 'necessary' condition of justification."

Annotated Sermon Summaries

Sermon 6: "The Righteousness of Faith"

Key Bible Verse(s): "For Moses describeth the righteousness which is of the law, That the man which doeth those things shall live by them. But the righteousness which is of faith speaketh on this wise, say not in thine heart, Who shall ascend into heaven? (that is, to bring Christ down from above:) Or, who shall descend into the deep? (that is, to bring up Christ again from the dead) But what saith it? The word is nigh thee, even in thy mouth, and in thy heart: that is, the word of faith, which we preach" (Romans 10:5–8).

Summary: In this lesson, Wesley first speaks of what the Law is, and then explains the difference between the righteousness of the law and the righteousness of faith—specifically, why the law is folly and faith sublime.

Main Themes: Righteousness, Law, and Obedience

Key Quotations and Passages:

- "[R]equired that man should fulfill all righteousness, inward and outward, negative and positive: That he should not only abstain from every idle word, and avoid every evil work, but should keep every affection, every desire, every thought, in obedience to the will of God."

- "[I]s that method of reconciliation with God which hath been chosen and established by God himself, not only as he is the God of wisdom, but as he is the sovereign Lord of heaven and earth, and of every creature which he hath made."

- "The covenant of works, in order to man's continuance in the favour of God, in his knowledge and love, in holiness and happiness, required of perfect man a perfect and uninterrupted obedience to every point of the law of God. Whereas, the covenant of grace, in order to man's recovery of the favour and the life of God, requires only faith; living faith in Him who, through God, justifies him that obeyed not."

Sermon 7: "The Way to the Kingdom"

Key Bible Verse(s): "And saying, the time is fulfilled, and the kingdom of God is at hand: repent ye, and believe the gospel" (Mark 1:15).

Summary: In this message, Wesley seeks to enlighten his listeners regarding the way of true religion.

Main Themes: Kingdom of God, Heart, The Way, Belief, and Grace

Key Quotations and Passages:

- "The nature of religion is so far from consisting in these, in forms of worship, or rites and ceremonies, that it does not properly consist in any outward actions, of what kind so ever."
- "[O]r a heart right toward God and man, implies happiness as well as holiness."
- "[R]epentance, this faith, this peace, joy, love, this change from glory to glory."

Sermon 8: "The First Fruits of the Spirit"

Key Bible Verse(s): "There is therefore now no condemnation to them which are in Christ Jesus, who walk not after the flesh, but after the Spirit" (Romans 8:1).

Summary: In this discourse, Wesley provides insight into the characteristics that a real Christian should demonstrate and the assurance of salvation they can experience.

Main Themes: Christian Characteristics, Freedom, Self-control, and Patience

Key Quotations and Passages:

- "Being filled with faith and with the Holy Ghost, they possess in their hearts, and show forth in their lives, in the whole course of their words and actions, the genuine fruits of the Spirit of God, namely, 'love, joy, peace, long-suffering, gentleness, goodness, fidelity, meekness, temperance,' and whatsoever else is lovely or praiseworthy."

- "For so long as they believe, and walk after the Spirit, neither God condemns them, nor their own heart."
- "The rule which some give, as to wilful sins, and which, in that case, may perhaps be dangerous, is undoubtedly wise and safe if it be applied only to the case of weakness and infirmities."

Sermon 9: "The Spirit of Bondage and of Adoption"

Key Bible Verse(s): "For ye have not received the spirit of bondage again to fear; but ye have received the Spirit of adoption, whereby we cry, Abba, Father" (Romans 8:15).

Summary: In his sermon, Wesley hopes to assist his hearers in coming to an honest understanding about the state of their relationship with God.

Main Themes: Natural Man, The Law, Grace, and Reality

Key Quotations and Passages:

- "His spiritual senses are not awake; they discern neither spiritual good nor evil."
- "He is a willing servant of sin, content with the bondage of corruption; inwardly and outwardly unholy, and satisfied therewith."
- "He cannot fear any longer the wrath of God; for he knows it is now turned away from him, and looks upon Him no more as an angry Judge, but as a loving Father."
- "[T]he Christian enjoys the true glorious liberty of the sons of God."

Sermon 10: "The Witness of the Spirit, Discourse I"

Key Bible Verse(s): "The Spirit itself beareth witness with our spirit, that we are the children of God" (Romans 8:16).

Summary: In this message, Wesley sets forth to describe the hallmarks so that people may know if they are indeed an authentic Christian.

Main Themes: Enthusiasm, Spirit, and Truth

Key Quotations and Passages:

- "How does it appear, that we do love God and our neighbour, and that we keep his commandments? Observe, that the meaning of the question is, How does it appear to ourselves, not to others?"

- "It is a consciousness of our having received, in and by the Spirit of adoption, the tempers mentioned in the Word of God as belonging to his adopted children; even a loving heart toward God and toward all mankind."

- "The soul as intimately and evidently perceives when it loves, delights, and rejoices in God, as when it loves and delights in anything on earth."

- "The immediate fruits of the Spirit ruling in the heart, are 'love, joy, peace, bowels of mercies, humbleness of mind, meekness, gentleness, long-suffering.' [Gal. 5:22, 23] And the outward fruits are, the doing good to all men; the doing no evil to any; and the walking in the light, [1 John 1:7]—a zealous, uniform obedience to all the commandments of God."

Sermon 11: "The Witness of the Spirit, Discourse II"

Key Bible Verse(s): "For our rejoicing is this, the testimony of our conscience, that in simplicity and godly sincerity, not with fleshly wisdom, but by the grace of God, we have had our conversation in the world, and more abundantly to you-ward" (2 Corinthians 1:12).

Summary: Discourse II is an extrapolation and defense of Wesley's first sermon on the Witness of the Spirit.

Main Themes: Doctrine, Spirit of God, Spirit of Man, Scripture, and Witness

Key Quotations and Passages:

- "The testimony of the Spirit is an inward impression on the souls of believers, whereby the Spirit of God directly testifies to their spirit, that they are children of God."
- "The true witness of the Spirit is known by its fruit, 'love, peace, joy;' not indeed preceding, but following it."
- "[B]y the experience of all who are convinced of sin, who can never rest till they have a direct witness; and even of the children of the world, who, not having the witness in themselves, one and all declare, none can know his sins forgiven."

Sermon 12: "The Witness of Our Own Spirit"

Key Bible Verse(s): "For our rejoicing is this, the testimony of our conscience, that in simplicity and godly sincerity, not with fleshly wisdom, but by the grace of God, we have had our conversation in the world, and more abundantly to you-ward" (2 Corinthians 1:12).

Summary: In this sermon, Wesley seeks to explain what the nature and basis for the joy Christians claim to experience.

Main Themes: Conscience, Self-awareness, Sincerity, and Joy

Key Quotations and Passages:

- "[A] faculty or power, implanted by God in every soul that comes into the world, of perceiving what is right or wrong in his own heart or life, in his tempers, thoughts, words, and actions."

- "[I]s a lantern unto a Christian's feet, and a light in all his paths."
- "[A] steady view, a single intention of promoting his glory, of doing and suffering his blessed will, runs through our whole soul, fills all our heart, and is the constant spring of all our thoughts, desires, and purposes."
- "I rejoice, because the sense of God's love to me hath, by the same Spirit, wrought in me to love him, and to love for his sake every child of man, every soul that he hath made."

Sermon 13: "On Sin in Believers"

Key Bible Verse(s): "Therefore if any man be in Christ, he is a new creature: old things are passed away; behold, all things are become new" (2 Corinthians 5:17).

Summary: Wesley tries to explain that every Christian battles within themself on whether God or sin will reign inside their heart. Holiness, then, is a matter of degrees and every believer has to continually work towards purifying themselves.

Main Themes: Sin, Regeneration, Scripture, and Correct Doctrine

Key Quotations and Passages:

- "Indeed some of these seem to carry the thing too far; so describing the corruption of heart in a believer, as scarce to allow that he has dominion over it, but rather is in bondage thereto; and, by this means, they leave hardly any distinction between a believer and an unbeliever."
- "By sin, I here understand inward sin; any sinful temper, passion, or affection; such as pride, self-will, love of the world,

in any kind or degree; such as lust, anger, peevishness; any disposition contrary to the mind which was in Christ."

- "[T]here are two contrary principles in believers—nature and grace, the flesh and the Spirit, runs through all the Epistles of St. Paul, yea, through all the Holy Scriptures."
- "Christ indeed cannot reign, where sin reigns; neither will he dwell where any sin is allowed. But he is and dwells in the heart of every believer, who is fighting against all sin; although it be not yet purified, according to the purification of the sanctuary."

Sermon 14: "The Repentance of Believers"

Key Bible Verse(s): "And saying, the time is fulfilled, and the kingdom of God is at hand: repent ye, and believe the gospel" (Mark 1:15).

Summary: This sermon points out that our salvation is not so simple after all. It requires not only an acknowledgment of personal sin, but also a motivating conviction to be free of sin in human hearts.

Main Themes: Repentance, Faith, and Sin

Key Quotations and Passages:

- "[T]his repentance and faith are full as necessary, in order to our continuance and growth in grace, as the former faith and repentance were, in order to our entering into the kingdom of God."
- "Now self-will, as well as pride, is a species of idolatry and both are directly contrary to the love of God."
- "The conviction of which is another branch of the repentance which belongs to them that are justified."
- "Thus it is, that in the children of God, repentance and faith exactly answer each other. By repentance we feel the sin

remaining in our hearts, and cleaving to our words and actions: by faith, we receive the power of God in Christ, purifying our hearts, and cleansing our hands."

Sermon 15: "The Great Assize"

Key Bible Verse(s): "But why dost thou judge thy brother? or why dost thou set at nought thy brother? for we shall all stand before the judgment seat of Christ" (Romans 14:10).

Summary: This message discusses the great judgment all people will eventually endure as well as the factors that precede and follow after it.

Location & Date: St. Paul's Church, Bedford; March 10, 1758

Main Themes: Judgmentalism, Order, Nature, and Conscience

Key Quotations and Passages:

- "The person by whom God will judge the world, is his only-begotten Son."
- "Every man, every woman, every infant of days, that ever breathed the vital air, will then hear the voice of the Son of God, and start into life, and appear before him."
- "So shall it be clearly and infallibly seen, who was righteous, and who unrighteous; and in what degree every action, or person, or character was either good or evil."
- "After the righteous are judged, the King will turn to them upon his left hand; and they shall also be judged, every man according to his works."
- "[N]ew heavens and a new earth."

Sermon 16: "The Means of Grace"

Key Bible Verse(s): "Even from the days of your fathers ye are gone away from mine ordinances, and have not kept them. Return unto me, and I will return unto you, saith the Lord of hosts. But ye said, wherein shall we return?" (Malachi 3:7).

Summary: Wesley focuses on the foundation for much of his theology (grace) and imparts how it is obtained and utilized.

Main Themes: Grace, Authenticity, and Salvation

Key Quotations and Passages:

- "[T]he things which should have been for their health, were to them an occasion of falling."
- "By 'means of grace' I understand outward signs, words, or actions, ordained of God, and appointed for this end, to be the ordinary channels whereby he might convey to men, preventing, justifying, or sanctifying grace."
- "[T]hat it is the blood of Christ alone, whereby any sinner can be reconciled to God; there being no other propitiation for our sins, no other fountain for sin and uncleanness."
- "Ye are thus saved, not by any power, wisdom, or strength, which is in you, or in any other creature; but merely through the grace or power of the Holy Ghost, which worketh all in all."
- "[T]his is a means whereby God not only gives, but also confirms and increases, true wisdom."

Sermon 17: "The Circumcision of the Heart"

Key Bible Verse(s): "But he is a Jew, which is one inwardly; and circumcision is that of the heart, in the spirit, and not in the letter; whose praise is not of men, but of God" (Romans 2:29).

Summary: Wesley goes about explaining the right state of mind, soul, and spirit with God, and the impact that has on the Believer's life.

Location & Date: St. Mary's, Oxford; January 1, 1733

Main Themes: Ignorance, Soul, and Conviction

Key Quotations and Passages:

- "[T]hat circumcision of the heart . . . is that habitual disposition of soul which, in the sacred writings, is termed holiness; and which directly implies, the being cleansed from sin"
- "[T]hat faith which alone is able to make them whole, which is the one medicine given under heaven to heal their sickness."
- "Whatever ye desire or fear, whatever ye seek or shun, whatever ye think, speak, or do, be it in order to your happiness in God, the sole End, us well as Source, of your being."

Sermon 18: "The Marks of the New Birth"

Key Bible Verse(s): "The wind bloweth where it listeth, and thou hearest the sound thereof, but canst not tell whence it cometh, and whither it goeth: so is every one that is born of the Spirit" (John 3:8).

Summary: Wesley elaborates on what it means to be born again as a child of God and having the spirit of adoption.

Main Themes: New Birth, Faith, Hope, and Love

Key Quotations and Passages:

- "The true, living, Christian faith, which whosoever hath, is born of God, is not only an assent, an act of the understanding; but a disposition, which God hath wrought in his heart."

- "An immediate and constant fruit of this faith whereby we are born of God . . . is power over sin."
- "Another fruit of this living faith is peace."
- "A Second scriptural mark of those who are born of God, is hope."
- "A Third scriptural mark of those who are born of God, and the greatest of all, is love."

Sermon 19: "The Great Privilege of Those That Are Born of God"

Key Bible Verse(s): "Whosoever is born of God doth not commit sin; for his seed remaineth in him: and he cannot sin, because he is born of God" (1 John 3:9).

Summary: Wesley discusses what is meant by being "born of God," and how that enables the Christian not to commit sin.

Main Themes: Justification, Regeneration, Sin, and The Fall

Key Quotations and Passages:

- "[I]t implies not barely the being baptized, or any outward change whatever; but a vast inward change, a change wrought in the soul, by the operation of the Holy Ghost; a change in the whole manner of our existence; for, from the moment we are born of God, we live in quite another manner than we did before; we are, as it were, in another world."
- "And by this new kind of spiritual respiration, spiritual life is not only sustained, but increased day by day, together with spiritual strength, and motion, and sensation; all the senses of the soul being now awake, and capable of discerning spiritual good and evil."
- "[W]hat the life of God in the soul of a believer is immediately and necessarily implies the continual inspiration of God's Holy Spirit."

Sermon 20: "The Lord Our Righteousness"

Key Bible Verse(s): "In his days Judah shall be saved, and Israel shall dwell safely: and this is his name whereby he shall be called, The Lord Our Righteousness" (Jeremiah 23:6).

Summary: Wesley ruminates, attempting to show what the righteousness of God is, how it affects humanity, and the consequences of it in Christian life.

Location & Date: Chapel in West-Street, 7 Dials; November 24, 1765

Main Themes: Controversy, Righteousness, Devotion, and Imputation

Key Quotations and Passages:

- "Now this is his eternal, essential, immutable holiness; his infinite justice, mercy, and truth; in all which, he and the Father are One."
- "The whole and every part of his obedience was complete."
- "Men may differ from us in their opinions, as well as their expressions, and nevertheless be partakers with us of the same precious faith."
- "But is not a believer invested or clothed with the righteousness of Christ? Undoubtedly he is."

Sermon 21: "Upon Our Lord's Sermon on the Mount"

Key Bible Verse(s): "And seeing the multitudes, he went up into a mountain: and when he was set, his disciples came unto him: And he opened his mouth, and taught them, saying, Blessed are the poor in spirit: for theirs is the kingdom of heaven. Blessed are they that mourn: for they shall be comforted" (Matthew 5:1–4).

Summary: Wesley extrapolates on Jesus' words in his great application of the faith, and shows their application to Christians and the living out of what they believe.

Main Themes: True Religion, Intention, and Stumbling Blocks

Key Quotations and Passages:

- "The Son of God, who came from heaven, is here showing us the way to heaven; to the place which he hath prepared for us; the glory he had before the world began."
- "[E]ither all the parts of this discourse are to be applied to men in general, or no part; seeing they are all connected together, all joined as the stones in an arch, of which you cannot take one away, without destroying the whole fabric."
- "Sinner, awake! Know thyself!"

Sermon 22: "Upon our Lord's Sermon on the Mount: Discourse 2"

Key Bible Verse(s): "Blessed are the meek: for they shall inherit the earth. Blessed are they which do hunger and thirst after righteousness: for they shall be filled. Blessed are the merciful: for they shall obtain mercy" (Matthew 5:5–7).

Summary: This is a continuation of the examination of the Sermon on the Mount. Wesley focuses a great deal on the necessity of love for neighbors and what that commandment truly requires.

Main Themes: Meekness, Charity, and Righteousness

Key Quotations and Passages:

- "He warns us, that the performing our duty to God will not excuse us from our duty to our neighbor."

- "Such is pride, the first, grand hindrance of all religion, which is taken away by poverty of spirit; levity and thoughtlessness, which prevent any religion from taking root in the soul, till they are removed by holy mourning; such are anger, impatience, discontent, which are all healed by Christian meekness."
- "It [charity] suffers all the weakness, ignorance, errors, infirmities, all the forwardness and littleness of faith, of the children of God; all the malice and wickedness of the children of the world."
- "And the more they are filled with the life of God, the more tenderly will they be concerned for those who are still without God in the world, still dead in trespasses and sins."

Sermon 23: "Upon our Lord's Sermon on the Mount: Discourse 3"

Key Bible Verse(s): "Blessed are the pure in heart: for they shall see God. Blessed are the peacemakers: for they shall be called the children of God. Blessed are they which are persecuted for righteousness' sake: for theirs is the kingdom of heaven. Blessed are ye, when men shall revile you, and persecute you, and shall say all manner of evil against you falsely, for my sake. Rejoice, and be exceeding glad: for great is your reward in heaven: for so persecuted they the prophets which were before you" (Matthew 5:8–12).

Summary: Wesley continues with his examination of Beatitudes with some exhortations to holiness, to courage, and to consistency.

Main Themes: Purity, Peacefulness, Persecution, and Joy

Key Quotations and Passages:

- "They are, through the power of his grace, purified from pride, by the deepest poverty of spirit; from anger, from every unkind or turbulent passion, by meekness and gentleness; from every desire but to please and enjoy God, to know and love him more and more, by that hunger and thirst after righteousness which now engrosses their whole soul: So that now they love the Lord their God with all their heart, and with all their soul, and mind, and strength."

- "[T]he great lesson which our blessed Lord inculcates here, and which he illustrates by this example, is, that God is in all things, and that we are to see the Creator in the glass of every creature; that we should use and look upon nothing as separate from God, which indeed is a kind of practical atheism; but, with a true magnificence of thought, survey heaven and earth, and all that is therein, as contained by God in the hollow of his hand, who by his intimate presence holds them all in being, who pervades and actuates the whole created frame, and is, in a true sense, the soul of universe."

- "The spirit which is in the world is directly opposite to the Spirit which is of God."

Sermon 24:
"Upon our Lord's Sermon on the Mount: Discourse 4"

Key Bible Verse(s): "Ye are the salt of the earth: but if the salt have lost his savour, wherewith shall it be salted? it is thenceforth good for nothing, but to be cast out, and to be trodden under foot of men. Ye are the light of the world. A city that is set on a hill cannot be hid. Neither do men light a candle, and put it under a bushel, but on a candlestick; and it giveth light unto all that are in the house. Let your light so shine before men, that they may see your good works, and glorify your Father which is in heaven" (Matthew 5:13–16).

Summary: This part of Wesley's examination dwells upon the role of Christianity as a social religion—one that takes part in and seeks to positively change the social environment around it.

Main Themes: Authenticity, Holiness, and Evangelism

Key Quotations and Passages:

- "The ornament of a meek, humble, loving spirit, will at least excite the approbation of all those who are capable in any degree, of discerning spiritual good and evil."
- "[I]t cannot subsist at all, without society—without living and conversing with other men."
- "Toward those who have never tasted of the good word, God is indeed pitiful and of tender mercy. But justice takes place with regard to those who have tasted that the Lord is gracious, and have afterwards turned back."
- "It is true, men who love darkness rather than light, because their deeds are evil, will take all possible pains to prove, that the light which is in you is darkness."

Sermon 25:
"Upon our Lord's Sermon on the Mount: Discourse 5"

Key Bible Verse(s): "Think not that I am come to destroy the law, or the prophets: I am not come to destroy, but to fulfil. For verily I say unto you, till heaven and earth pass, one jot or one tittle shall in no wise pass from the law, till all be fulfilled. Whosoever therefore shall break one of these least commandments, and shall teach men so, he shall be called the least in the kingdom of heaven: but whosoever shall do and teach them, the same shall be called great in the kingdom of heaven. For I say unto you, that except your righteousness shall exceed the righteousness of the scribes and Pharisees, ye shall in no case enter into the kingdom of heaven" (Matthew 5:17–20).

Summary: This sermon deals with Jesus' effect on the Jewish religion: was Jesus introducing a new religion or abolishing the old one or was he just fulfilling it?

Main Themes: Fulfillment, Commandments, and Righteousness

Key Quotations and Passages:

- "The moral stands on an entirely different foundation from the ceremonial or ritual law, which was only designed for a temporary restraint upon a disobedient and stiff-necked people."
- "[T]here is no contrariety at all between the law and the gospel."
- "Let thy soul be filled with mildness, gentleness, patience, long-suffering toward all men; at the same time that all which is in thee is athirst for God, the living God, longing to awake up after his likeness, and to be satisfied with it."

Sermon 26: "Upon our Lord's Sermon on the Mount: Discourse 6"

Key Bible Verse(s): "Take heed that ye do not [display] your alms before men, to be seen of them: otherwise ye have no reward of your Father which is in heaven. Therefore when thou doest thine alms, do not sound a trumpet before thee, as the hypocrites do in the synagogues and in the streets, that they may have glory of men. Verily I say unto you, they have their reward. But when thou doest alms, let not thy left hand know what thy right hand doeth: That thine alms may be in secret: and thy Father which seeth in secret himself shall reward thee openly. And when thou prayest, thou shalt not be as the hypocrites are: for they love to pray standing in the synagogues and in the corners of the streets, that they may be seen of men. Verily I say unto you, they have their reward. But thou, when thou prayest, enter into thy closet, and when thou hast shut thy door, pray to thy Father which is in secret; and thy Father which seeth in secret shall reward thee openly. But when ye pray, use not vain repetitions, as the heathen do: for they think that they shall be heard for their much speaking. Be not ye therefore like unto them: for your Father knoweth what things ye have need of, before ye ask him. After this manner therefore pray ye: Our Father which art in heaven, Hallowed be thy name. Thy kingdom come, Thy will be done in earth, as it is in heaven. Give us this day our daily bread. And forgive us our debts, as we forgive our debtors. And lead us not into temptation, but deliver us from evil: For thine is the kingdom, and the power, and the glory, for ever. Amen. For if ye forgive men their trespasses, your heavenly Father will also forgive you: But if ye forgive not men their trespasses, neither will your Father forgive your trespasses" (Matthew 6:1–15).

Summary: This is a comprehensive breakdown of the Lord's Prayer, focusing on healthy attitudes and avoiding vanity of heart and actions.

Main Themes: Humbleness, Good Intentions, Reverence, and Honesty

Key Quotations and Passages:

- "He proceeds to show, in this chapter, how all our actions likewise, even those that are indifferent in their own nature, may be made holy, and good and acceptable to God, by a pure and holy intention."
- "Purity of intention is equally destroyed by a view to any temporal reward whatever."

- "[O]ur prayers are the proper test of our desires; nothing being fit to have a place in our desires which is not fit to have a place in our prayers: What we may not pray for, neither should we desire."

Sermon 27: "Upon our Lord's Sermon on the Mount: Discourse 7"

Key Bible Verse(s): "Moreover when ye fast, be not, as the hypocrites, of a sad countenance: for they disfigure their faces, that they may appear unto men to fast. Verily I say unto you, they have their reward. But thou, when thou fastest, anoint thine head, and wash thy face; That thou appear not unto men to fast, but unto thy Father which is in secret: and thy Father, which seeth in secret, shall reward thee openly" (Matthew 6:16–18).

Summary: Wesley goes into detail about the nature, practices, limitations, and benefits of fasting.

Main Themes: Hypocrisy, Pride, Fasting, Abstinence, and Reward

Key Quotations and Passages:

- "As to the degrees or measures of fasting, we have instances of some who have fasted several days together."
- "Here is another perpetual reason for fasting; to remove the food of lust and sensuality, to withdraw the incentives of foolish and hurtful desires, of vile and vain affections."
- "And it is a means not only of turning away the wrath of God, but also of obtaining whatever blessings we stand in need of."
- "Let us beware of mocking God, of turning our fast, as well as our prayers, into an abomination unto the Lord, by the mixture of any temporal view, particularly by seeking the praise of men."

Sermon 28:
"Upon our Lord's Sermon on the Mount: Discourse 8"

Key Bible Verse(s): "Lay not up for yourselves treasures upon earth, where moth and rust doth corrupt, and where thieves break through and steal: But lay up for yourselves treasures in heaven, where neither moth nor rust doth corrupt, and where thieves do not break through nor steal: For where your treasure is, there will your heart be also. The light of the body is the eye: if therefore thine eye be single, thy whole body shall be full of light. But if thine eye be evil, thy whole body shall be full of darkness. If therefore the light that is in thee be darkness, how great is that darkness!" (Matthew 6:19–23).

Summary: Wesley expands upon the Christian notion of the Two Kingdoms.

Main Themes: Vanity, Investment, Appreciation, and Reality

Key Quotations and Passages:

- "If you aim at 'laying up treasures on earth,' you are not barely losing your time and spending your strength for that which is not bread: for what is the fruit if you succeed?—You have murdered your own soul!"

- "Weigh thyself in another balance: estimate thyself only by the measure of faith and love which God hath given thee."

- "A vast majority of them are under a curse, under the peculiar curse of God; inasmuch as in the general tenor of their lives they are not only robbing God continually, embezzling and wasting their Lord's goods, and by that very means corrupting their own souls; but also robbing the poor, the hungry, the naked, wronging the widow and the fatherless, and making themselves accountable for all the want, affliction, and distress which they may but do not remove."

Sermon 29:
"Upon our Lord's Sermon on the Mount: Discourse 9"

Key Bible Verse(s): "No man can serve two masters: for either he will hate the one, and love the other; or else he will hold to the one, and despise the other. Ye cannot serve God and mammon. Therefore I say unto you, Take no thought for your life, what ye shall eat, or what ye shall drink; nor yet for your body, what ye shall put on. Is not the life more than meat, and the body than raiment? Behold the fowls of the air: for they sow not, neither do they reap, nor gather into barns; yet your heavenly Father feedeth them. Are ye not much better than they? Which of you by taking thought can add one cubit unto his stature? And why take ye thought for raiment? Consider the lilies of the field, how they grow; they toil not, neither do they spin: And yet I say unto you, That even Solomon in all his glory was not arrayed like one of these. Wherefore, if God so clothe the grass of the field, which to day is, and to morrow is cast into the oven, shall he not much more clothe you, O ye of little faith? Therefore take no thought, saying, What shall we eat? or, What shall we drink? or, Wherewithal shall we be clothed? (For after all these things do the Gentiles seek:) for your heavenly Father knoweth that ye have need of all these things. But seek ye first the kingdom of God, and his righteousness; and all these things shall be added unto you. Take therefore no thought for the morrow: for the morrow shall take thought for the things of itself. Sufficient unto the day is the evil thereof" (Matthew 6:24–34).

Summary: Wesley attempts to enlighten his audience regarding the realities of serving God versus other idols in daily living.

Main Themes: Loyalty, Trust, Worry, Prioritization, and Maturity

Key Quotations and Passages:

- "It implies, to trust in God as our happiness; as the centre of spirits; the only rest of our souls; the only good who is adequate to all our capacities, and sufficient to satisfy all the desires he hath given us."

- "It is good and acceptable to God, that we should so take thought concerning whatever we have in hand, as to have a clear comprehension of what we are about to do, and to plan our business before we enter upon it."

- "Let God have the sole dominion over you: Let him reign without a rival: Let him possess all your heart, and rule alone."

Sermon 30:
"Upon our Lord's Sermon on the Mount: Discourse 10"

Key Bible Verse(s): "Judge not, that ye be not judged. For with what judgment ye judge, ye shall be judged: and with what measure ye mete, it shall be measured to you again. And why beholdest thou the mote that is in thy brother's eye, but considerest not the beam that is in thine own eye? Or how wilt thou say to thy brother, Let me pull out the mote out of thine eye; and, behold, a beam is in thine own eye? Thou hypocrite, first cast out the beam out of thine own eye; and then shalt thou see clearly to cast out the mote out of thy brother's eye. Give not that which is holy unto the dogs, neither cast ye your pearls before swine, lest they trample them under their feet, and turn again and rend you. Ask, and it shall be given you; seek, and ye shall find; knock, and it shall be opened unto you: For every one that asketh receiveth; and he that seeketh findeth; and to him that knocketh it shall be opened. Or what man is there of you, whom if his son ask bread, will he give him a stone? Or if he ask a fish, will he give him a serpent? If ye then, being evil, know how to give good gifts unto your children, how much more shall your Father which is in heaven give good things to them that ask him? Therefore all things whatsoever ye would that men should do to you, do ye even so to them: for this is the law and the prophets" (Matthew 7:1–12).

Summary: Wesley advocates a careful approach to dealing with conflicts; specifically, in the area of judging, he admonishes his listeners to let mercy and truth govern justice in their lives.

Main Themes: Judging, Hypocrisy, Openness, and Faith

Key Quotations and Passages:

- "They spend their time in finding out their neighbour's faults, instead of amending their own."
- "The thinking of another in a manner that is contrary to love is that judging which is here condemned."
- "This is that royal law, that golden rule of mercy as well as justice, which even the heathen Emperor caused to be written over the gate of his palace; a rule which many believe to be naturally engraved on the mind of everyone that comes into the world."
- "Let justice, mercy, and truth govern all our minds and actions."[/BL]

Sermon 31:
"Upon our Lord's Sermon on the Mount: Discourse 11"

Key Bible Verse(s): "Enter ye in at the strait gate: for wide is the gate, and broad is the way, that leadeth to destruction, and many there be which go in thereat: Because strait is the gate, and narrow is the way, which leadeth unto life, and few there be that find it" (Matthew 7:13–14).

Summary: Wesley focuses on the exclusive, non-universalism reality of salvation for all people, suggesting that there is a specific holy path of God for humanity to follow despite what the godless suggest.

Main Themes: Dangers, Exclusivity, and Caution

Key Quotations and Passages:

- "Wide indeed is the gate, and broad the way, that leadeth to destruction! For sin is the gate of hell, and wickedness the way to destruction."

- "Yea, the higher they are raised in fortune and power, the deeper do they sink into wickedness. The more blessings they have received from God, the more sins do they commit; using their honour or riches, their learning or wisdom, not as means of working out their salvation, but rather of excelling in vice, and so insuring their own destruction!"

- "So narrow is the way that leadeth unto life, unto life everlasting—so strait the gate—that nothing unclean, nothing unholy, can enter."

- "Abstain from all appearance of evil: Do all possible good to all men: Deny thyself, thy own will, in all things, and take up thy cross daily. Be ready to cut off thy right hand, to pluck out thy right eye and cast it from thee; to suffer the loss of goods, friends, health, all things on earth, so thou mayst enter into the kingdom of heaven!"

Sermon 32:
"Upon our Lord's Sermon on the Mount: Discourse 12"

Key Bible Verse(s): "Beware of false prophets, which come to you in sheep's clothing, but inwardly they are ravening wolves. Ye shall know them by their fruits. Do men gather grapes of thorns, or figs of thistles? Even so every good tree bringeth forth good fruit; but a corrupt tree bringeth forth evil fruit. A good tree cannot bring forth evil fruit, neither can a corrupt tree bring forth good fruit. Every tree that bringeth not forth good fruit is hewn down, and cast into the fire. Wherefore by their fruits ye shall know them" (Matthew 7:15–20).

Summary: Wesley deals with the teachers of false and impure doctrine. He exhorts the listeners to be on guard and measure what they are hearing with the Word of God and warns the false prophets of the wrath they are storing up for themselves.

Main Themes: False prophets, Fruit, and Hard-heartedness

Key Quotations and Passages:

- "Those are false prophets, who teach a false way to heaven, a way which does not lead thither; or, (which comes in the end to the same point) who do not teach the true."
- "They come in the most mild, inoffensive manner, without any mark or token of enmity."
- "In like manner, a false prophet, one whom God hath not sent, does not bring forth evil fruit accidentally or sometimes only, but always, and of necessity."
- "Hear with fervent and continual prayer to Him who alone teacheth man wisdom."

Sermon 33:
"Upon our Lord's Sermon on the Mount: Discourse 13"

Key Bible Verse(s): "Not every one that saith unto me, Lord, Lord, shall enter into the kingdom of heaven; but he that doeth the will of my Father which is in heaven. Many will say to me in that day, Lord, Lord, have we not prophesied in thy name? and in thy name have cast out devils? and in thy name done many wonderful works? And then will I profess unto them, I never knew you:

depart from me, ye that work iniquity. Therefore, whosoever heareth these sayings of mine, and doeth them, I will liken him unto a wise man, which built his house upon a rock: And the rain descended, and the floods came, and the winds blew, and beat upon that house; and it fell not: for it was founded upon a rock. And every one that heareth these sayings of mine, and doeth them not, shall be likened unto a foolish man, which built his house upon the sand: And the rain descended, and the floods came, and the winds blew, and beat upon that house; and it fell: and great was the fall of it" (Matthew 7:21–27).

Summary: In this sermon, Wesley asserts what is a valid and invalid foundation of religion—one is built on sand; the other, the rock of salvation.

Main Themes: Shallowness, Foolishness, and Self-deception

Key Quotations and Passages:

- "For how far short is all this of that righteousness and true holiness which he has described therein! How widely distant from that inward kingdom of heaven which is now opened in the believing soul."

- "He is conscious of his lost estate, of the wrath of God abiding on him, and of his utter inability to help himself, till he is filled with peace and joy in the Holy Ghost."

- "How nearly then does it concern every child of man, practically to apply these things to himself! Diligently to examine on what foundation he builds, whether on a rock or on the sand!"

- "In a word: Let thy religion be the religion of the heart."

Sermon 34:
"The Original, Nature, Property, and Use of the Law"

Key Bible Verse(s): "Wherefore the law is holy, and the commandment holy, and just, and good" (Romans 7:12).

Summary: Wesley examines the moral law that Christians are to follow, what it is comprised of, and how to apply that Holy Law to our lives.

Main Themes: The Law, Beneficence, and Usefulness

Key Quotations and Passages:

- "[H]e gave to this free, intelligent creature the same law as to his first-born children,—not wrote, indeed, upon tables of stone, or any corruptible substance, but engraven on his heart by the finger of God; wrote in the inmost spirit both of men and of angels; to the intent it might never be far off, never hard to be understood, but always at hand, and always shining with clear light, even as the sun in the midst of heaven."

- "[T]he law of God in another point of view, it is supreme, unchangeable reason; it is unalterable rectitude, it is the everlasting fitness of all things that are or ever were created."

- "The law, then, is right and just concerning all things."

- "And the First use of it, without question, is, to convince the world of sin."

Sermon 35:
"The Law Established Through Faith: Discourse I"

Key Bible Verse(s): "Do we then make void the law through faith? God forbid: yea, we establish the law" (Romans 3:31).

Summary: In this message, Wesley attempts to put in proper perspective the relationship between law and faith, basically stating that faith without works is no faith at all and useless.

Main Themes: The Gospel, Salvation, Faith, and Process

Key Quotations and Passages:

- "It was easy to foresee an objection which might be made, and which has in fact been made in all ages; namely, that to say we are justified without the works of the law, is to abolish the law."
- "[T]o preach Christ, is to preach all things that Christ hath spoken; all his promises; all his threatenings and commands; all that is written in his book; and then you will know how to preach Christ, without making void the law."
- "The free grace of God, through the merits of Christ, gives pardon to them that believe; that believe with such a faith as, working by love, produces all obedience and holiness."

Sermon 36: "The Law Established Through Faith: Discourse II"

Key Bible Verse(s): "Do we then make void the law through faith? God forbid: yea, we establish the law" (Romans 3:31).

Summary: This sermon continues with his discourse on the value of faith for promoting righteousness and holiness. Love is the driving force but faith is the vehicle.

Main Themes: The Law, Awareness, and Contrivance

Key Quotations and Passages:

- "We establish the law, First, by our doctrine; by endeavouring to preach it in its whole extent, to explain and enforce every part of it, in the same manner as our great Teacher did while upon earth."

- "We establish the law, Secondly, when we so preach faith in Christ as not to supersede, but produce holiness; to produce all manner of holiness, negative and positive, of the heart and of the life."
- "Faith, then, was originally designed of God to re-establish the law of love."
- "[T]he most important way of establishing the law; namely, the establishing it in our own hearts and lives."
- "Let but the eye of the soul be constantly fixed, not on the things which are temporal, but on those which are eternal, and our affections are more and more loosened from earth, and fixed on things above."

Sermon 37: "The Nature of Enthusiasm"

Key Bible Verse(s): "And as he thus spake for himself, Festus said with a loud voice, Paul, thou art beside thyself; much learning doth make thee mad" (Acts 26:24).

Summary: Wesley examines the label that many placed upon him personally and his movement—"Enthusiasm." With an ironic sense of double play, he systematically breaks down the different types of enthusiasms that exist and their inherent dangers and, in the end, differentiates his movement from others.

Main Themes: Enthusiasm, Superficiality, Zeal, and Pride

Key Quotations and Passages:

- "Some take it in a good sense, for a divine impulse or impression, superior to all the natural faculties, and suspending, for the time, either in whole or in part, both the reason and the outward senses."

- "As to the nature of enthusiasm, it is, undoubtedly a disorder of the mind; and such a disorder as greatly hinders the exercise of reason."
- "But the most common of all the enthusiasts of this kind are those who imagine themselves Christians, and are not."

Sermon 38: "A Caution Against Bigotry"

Key Bible Verse(s): "And John answered him, saying, Master, we saw one casting out devils in thy name, and he followeth not us: and we forbad him, because he followeth not us. But Jesus said, Forbid him not: for there is no man which shall do a miracle in my name, that can lightly speak evil of me" (Mark 9:38–39).

Summary: This sermon deals with the issue of the spiritual side of life, freedom from spiritual powers, and freedom from arrogance and self-righteousness.

Main Themes: Bias, Snobbery, and Self-protection

Key Quotations and Passages:

- "By the power of God attending his word, he brings these sinners to repentance; an entire inward as well as outward change, from all evil to all good. And this is, in a sound sense, to cast out devils, out of the souls wherein they had hitherto dwelt."
- "Many there will necessarily be, in different parts of the harvest, so far from having any mutual intercourse, that they will be as absolute strangers to each other as if they had lived in different ages."
- "Do not in any wise strive to prevent his using all the power which God has given him."

- "Take care (1) That you do not convict yourself of bigotry, by your unreadiness to believe that any man does cast out devils, who differs from you."

Sermon 39: "Catholic Spirit"

Key Bible Verse(s): "And when he was departed thence, he lighted on Jehonadab the son of Rechab coming to meet him: and he saluted him, and said to him, Is thine heart right, as my heart is with thy heart? And Jehonadab answered, It is. If it be, give me thine hand. And he gave him his hand; and he took him up to him into the chariot" (2 Kings 10:15).

Summary: This message confronts the issues of controversy and contentiousness among God's people. Wesley advocates for a loving, tolerant acceptance that people will often have differing opinions, but that, with love and understanding, a congenial spirit may still be present.

Main Themes: Spiritual Health, Conscience, Love and Inspiration, and Universal Brotherhood

Key Quotations and Passages:

- "The two grand, general hindrances are, first, that they cannot all think alike and, in consequence of this, secondly, they cannot all walk alike."
- "It is an unavoidable consequence of the present weakness and shortness of human understanding, that several men will be of several minds in religion as well as in common life."
- "But every one must follow the dictates of his own conscience, in simplicity and godly sincerity."
- "[A] catholic spirit is not speculative latitudinarianism. It is not an indifference to all opinions: this is the spawn of hell, not the offspring of heaven."

- "He is the man of a truly catholic spirit, who bears all these continually upon his heart; who having an unspeakable tenderness for their persons, and longing for their welfare, does not cease to commend them to God in prayer, as well as to plead their cause before men; who speaks comfortably to them, and labours, by all his words, to strengthen their hands in God."

Sermon 40: "Christian Perfection"

Key Bible Verse(s): "Not as though I had already attained, either were already perfect: but I follow after, if that I may apprehend that for which also I am apprehended of Christ Jesus" (Philippians 3:12).

Summary: Always defending his controversial interpretation of Christian sanctification, Wesley presents the understanding of Christian Perfection.

Main Themes: Sanctification, Love, and Perfection

Key Quotations and Passages:

- "Christian perfection, therefore, does not imply (as some men seem to have imagined) an exemption either from ignorance or mistake, or infirmities or temptations."
- "[A]ll real Christians, or believers in Christ, are made free from outward sin."
- "He sinneth not willfully; or he doth not commit sin habitually; or, not as other men do; or, not as he did before."

Sermon 41: "Wandering Thoughts"

Key Bible Verse(s): "Casting down imaginations, and every high thing that exalteth itself against the knowledge of God, and bringing into captivity every thought to the obedience of Christ" (2 Corinthians 10:5).

Summary: Wesley presents what wandering thoughts are, what causes them, which are sinful or beneficial, and what are the consequences of them in Christian lives.

Main Themes: Unhealthy Thoughts, Temptations, and Moral & Intellectual Weakness

Key Quotations and Passages:

- "They are of two sorts: Thoughts that wander from God; and thoughts that wander from the particular point we have in hand."
- "[T]he occasion of the former sort of thoughts, which oppose or wander from God, are, in general, sinful tempers."
- "All thoughts which spring from sinful tempers, are undoubtedly sinful."
- "And then only, when we lie down in the dust, shall we be delivered from those wandering thoughts which are occasioned by what we see and hear, among those by whom we are now surrounded."
- "Rather let us pray, both with the spirit and with the understanding, that all these things may work together for our good."

Sermon 42: "Satan's Devices"

Key Bible Verse(s): "Lest Satan should get an advantage of us: for we are not ignorant of his devices" (2 Corinthians 2:11).

Summary: This sermon examines the nefarious, destructive work of the Devil against humanity, and how the Christian can successfully resist and defeat the ruler of the world.

Main Themes: Satan, Attacks, and Protection

Key Quotations and Passages:

- "He will endeavour to shake, yea, if it be possible, to destroy the holiness you have already received by your very expectation of receiving more, of attaining all the image of God."

- "At the same time that our wise adversary endeavours to make our conviction of the necessity of perfect love an occasion of shaking our peace by doubts and fears, he endeavours to weaken, if not destroy, our faith."

- "The more you are tempted to give up your shield, to cast away your faith, your confidence in his love, so much the more take heed that you hold fast that whereunto you have attained; so much the more labour to stir up the gift of God which is in you."

- "Improve the present moment. Buy up every opportunity of growing in grace, or of doing good."

Sermon 43: "The Scripture Way of Salvation"

Key Bible Verse(s): "For by grace are ye saved through faith; and that not of yourselves: it is the gift of God" (Ephesians 2:8).

Summary: Wesley explains what salvation is, how faith and justification are involved, and how it all works together for the good of the Christian.

Main Themes: Scripture, Salvation, Faith, and Exercise

Key Quotations and Passages:

- "It is not something at a distance: it is a present thing."

- "Justification is another word for pardon."

- "From the time of our being born again, the gradual work of sanctification takes place."

- "It implies both a supernatural evidence of God, and of the things of God; a kind of spiritual light exhibited to the soul, and a supernatural sight or perception thereof."

Sermon 44: "Original Sin"

Key Bible Verse(s): "And God saw that the wickedness of man was great in the earth, and that every imagination of the thoughts of his heart was only evil continually" (Genesis 6:5).

Summary: This discourse explains the state of humanity before Noah's Flood, its comparison to humanity in Wesley's era, and the importance of recognizing the reality of our dependence on God for everything.

Main Themes: Original Sin, Humanity, True Religion, and Healing

Key Quotations and Passages:

- "He [Noah] alone (perhaps including part of his household) was an exception from the universal wickedness, which, by the just judgment of God, in a short time after brought on universal destruction. All the rest were partakers in the same guilt, as they were in the same punishment."
- "No man loves God by nature, any more than he does a stone, or the earth he treads upon."
- "Indeed, if man were not thus fallen, there would be no need of all this. There would be no occasion for this work in the heart, this renewal in the spirit of our mind."

Sermon 45: "The New Birth"

Key Bible Verse(s): "Marvel not that I said unto thee, Ye must be born again" (John 3:7).

Summary: Wesley presents the purpose behind being born again, how it is accomplished, and to what glorious consequence(s).

Main Themes: Justification, Regeneration, New Birth, and Amazement

Key Quotations and Passages:

- "If any doctrines within the whole compass of Christianity may be properly termed fundamental, they are doubtless these two—the doctrine of justification, and that of the new birth."
- "The natural consequence of this is, that everyone descended from him comes into the world spiritually dead, dead to God, wholly dead in sin; entirely void of the life of God; void of the image of God, of all that righteousness and holiness wherein Adam was created."
- "A man may be born from above, born of God, born of the Spirit, in a manner which bears a very near analogy to the natural birth."
- "Of consequence, the new birth is absolutely necessary in order to [gain] eternal salvation."

Sermon 46: "The Wilderness State"

Key Bible Verse(s): "And ye now therefore have sorrow: but I will see you again, and your heart shall rejoice, and your joy no man taketh from you" (John 16:22).

Summary: This message seeks to describe what being in the wilderness means, what its causes are, and how to overcome it.

Main Themes: Spiritual Disease, Sin, Ignorance, Temptation, Despair, and Victory

Key Quotations and Passages:

- "It properly consists in the loss of that faith which God once wrought in their heart."
- "The most usual cause of inward darkness is sin, of one kind or another."
- "Another general cause of this darkness is ignorance."
- "A Third general cause of this darkness is temptation."
- "So long as men dream thus, they may well 'walk in darkness:' Nor can the effect cease, till the cause is removed."

Sermon 47: "Heaviness Through Manifold Temptations"

Key Bible Verse(s): "Wherein ye greatly rejoice, though now for a season, if need be, ye are in heaviness through manifold temptations" (1 Peter 1:6).

Summary: Wesley discusses the difficulty every person endures in life and gives hope that it is not in vain but ultimately exists to bring the creation closer to the creator.

Main Themes: Darkness, Heaviness, Grief, Trials, and Hope

Key Quotations and Passages:

- "The heaviness they were in was neither more nor less than sorrow or grief."
- "Hence we learn, that the first and great end of God's permitting the temptations which bring heaviness on his children, Is the trial of their faith, which is tried by these, even as gold by the fire."
- "They rejoice the more, because the trials which increase their faith and hope increase their love also; both their gratitude to God for all his mercies, and their goodwill to all mankind."
- "[T]here may be need of heaviness, but there can be no need of darkness."

Sermon 48: "Self-denial"

Key Bible Verse(s): "And he said to them all, If any man will come after me, let him deny himself, and take up his cross daily, and follow me" (Luke 9:23).

Summary: This is a vehement plea from Wesley that each Christian strive to take up their cross, deny their flesh, and follow God to perfection.

Main Themes: Appreciation, Self-denial, Submission, and Christ-Model

Key Quotations and Passages:

- "If we do not continually deny ourselves, we do not learn of Him, but of other masters. If we do not take up our cross daily, we do not come after Him, but after the world, or the prince of the world, or our own fleshly mind."
- "We see the nature of self-denial: It is the denying or refusing to follow our own will, from a conviction that the will of God is the only rule of action to us."
- "And every one that would follow Christ, that would be his real disciple, must not only deny himself, but take up his cross also. A cross is anything contrary to our will, anything displeasing to our nature."
- "[H]is faith is not made perfect, neither can he grow in grace; namely, because he will not deny himself, and take up his daily cross."

Sermon 49: "The Cure of Evil-speaking"

Key Bible Verse(s): "Moreover if thy brother shall trespass against thee, go and tell him his fault between thee and him alone: if he shall hear thee, thou hast gained thy brother. But if he will not hear thee, then take with thee one or two more, that in the mouth of two or three witnesses every word may be established. And if he shall neglect to hear them, tell it unto the church: but if he neglect to hear the church, let him be unto thee as an heathen man and a publican" (Matthew 18:15-17).

Summary: Wesley discusses the common problem of the evils of the tongue. His admonitions are biblically based and promote a loving, humble, yet resolute approach to dealing with slander and gossip.

Main Themes: Slander, Responsibility, and Altruism

Key Quotations and Passages:

- "For evil-speaking is neither more nor less than speaking evil of an absent person; relating something evil, which was really done or said by one that is not present when it is related."
- "Evil-speaking is the more difficult to be avoided, because it frequently attacks us in disguise."
- "Put ye away evil-speaking, talebearing, whispering: Let none of them proceed out of your mouth!"

Sermon 50: "The Use of Money"

Key Bible Verse(s): "And I say unto you, Make to yourselves friends of the mammon of unrighteousness; that, when ye fail, they may receive you into everlasting habitations" (Luke 16:9).

Summary: This sermon instructs listeners to the proper use of money and fortune, including its gain, savings, and dispensation, which are to incorporate a holy attitude of simplicity and love.

Main Themes: Money, Pride, Waste, Investment, and Wisdom

Key Quotations and Passages:

- "The fault does not lie in the money, but in them that use it."

- "We are. Thirdly, to gain all we can without hurting our neighbour."
- "Gain all you can, by common sense, by using in your business all the understanding which God has given you."
- "Brethren, can we be either wise or faithful stewards unless we thus manage our Lord's goods?"

Sermon 51: "The Good Steward"

Key Bible Verse(s): "And he saw also a certain poor widow casting in thither two mites" (Luke 21:2).

Summary: Wesley points out that everything humanity has is merely borrowed from God; therefore, people ought to use their time wisely in the service of God.

Main Themes: Stewardship, Kingdom, and Supererogation

Key Quotations and Passages:

- "For he is not the proprietor of any of these things, but barely entrusted with them by another."
- "[H]e hath entrusted us with our souls, our bodies, our goods, and whatever other talents we have received."
- "As the soul will retain its understanding and memory, notwithstanding the dissolution of the body, so undoubtedly the will, including all the affections, will remain in its full vigour."
- "I entrusted thee with an immortal spirit, endowed with various powers and faculties, with understanding, imagination, memory, will, affections. I gave thee withal full and express directions, how all these were to be employed. Didst thou employ thy understanding, as far as it was capable, according to those directions."

Sermon 52: "Reformation of Manners"

Key Bible Verse(s): "Who will rise up for me against the evildoers? or who will stand up for me against the workers of iniquity?" (Psalm 94:16).

Summary: This sermon urges the members of society to be loving, holy, and morally upright, and to demand and enforce the social code in their culture and communities.

Location & Date: Chapel in West-Street, 7 Dials; January 30, 1763

Main Themes: Self-control, Manners, Society, and Morality

Key Quotations and Passages:

- "[T]he Church of Christ. It is a body of men compacted together, in order, first, to save each his own soul; then to assist each other in working out their salvation; and, afterwards, as far as in them lies, to save all men from present and future misery, to overturn the kingdom of Satan, and set up the kingdom of Christ."

- "How excellent is the design to prevent in any degree the dishonour done to his glorious name, the contempt which is poured on his authority, and the scandal brought upon our holy religion by the gross, flagrant wickedness of those who are still called by the name of Christ!"

- "And if such a breach both of divine and human laws is not to be punished because a man is not convinced it is a sin, there is an end of all execution of justice, and all men may live as they list."

- "He that has faith and confidence in God, will, of consequence, be a man of courage."

4

Theological Reflections

READING THROUGH WESLEY'S ELABORATE sermons, crucial conclusions can be ascertained about the founder of the Methodist movement. First, Wesley was a sincerely devoted man of God and the scriptures. In reading his words, the profound love he has for God and his personal responsibility as a minister of God is evident. Moreover, based on his personal experiences and consistency of message, there appears to be no ulterior motives for Wesley other than to help people cultivate a closer relationship with God and others. One is reminded of the Apostle Paul's words in 2 Corinthians 4—"Therefore, since through God's mercy we have this ministry, we do not lose heart. Rather, we have renounced secret and shameful ways; we do not use deception, nor do we distort the word of God. On the contrary, by setting forth the truth plainly, we commend ourselves to everyone's conscience in the sight of God." In that way, Wesley talked and walked as a devoted child of the Father—the same Father who reached out and delivered people from their sin rescued him, too.

Second, Wesley was an admirable and capable biblical scholar. Hence, Deborah Madden writes,

> John Wesley's theological and literary productions are, by any standards, prodigious. Even within his lifetime, Wesley's output ran to thousands of pages, hundreds of

Theological Reflections

volumes, which included sermons, journals, tracts, edited abridgements, and numerous other commentaries.[1]

The plenitude of scripture and brilliant insights that he utilized in every sermon demonstrates his base of knowledge and interpretative skills.

At Oxford, "He mastered at least seven languages and developed a truly comprehensive outlook on all areas of investigation. His mind never closed to inquiry for the rest of his life."[2] To argue with Wesley must have been an arduous and daunting task, indeed. His ability to find cultural connections and solutions within scripture greatly aided his studies and theories and applications.

Third, key life experiences certainly shaped his approach to life and theology, although Wesley seemed perpetually in the refiner's fire. As Kenneth Collins writes, "Although the Epworth rectory played a salient role in Wesley's spiritual formation, it was relatively short lived."[3] From his dramatic upbringing to his "soap opera" ministerial duties at home and abroad to his being a provocative schoolmaster, after each experience, Wesley responded with purpose, reflection, and for improvement. This is not to imply that he had an unthinking, knee-jerk approach to theology—just that he applied his life to theology and vice versa.

This personal approach to "The Way" can be seen in his understanding of the Christian life process. A healthy and whole relationship with God begins with confession of one's sinfulness and a repentant heart. Instantly, the sinner is justified by his or her faith, and enjoys an ongoing regeneration of the soul. This bright flame of newfound spiritual recovery is fanned brighter through the nurturing of fellow believers (and former sinners) in smaller, intimate groups. As members work to achieve greater sanctification, their maturity grows as does their effectiveness as true, confident children of God. With a willing heart and the inseparable assistance of the Holy Spirit, he or she who was once lost can experience the

1. Madden, "Wesley as Advisor," 176.
2. Curtis, "John Wesley and Women," 9.
3. Collins, "Wesley's Life and Ministry," 43.

perfect love of God and neighbor. Such a conclusion may seem impossible to some (particularly to staunch Augustinians or Calvinists), but Wesley would gently remind them, "With men, this is impossible; but with God, all things are possible" (Matthew 19:26).

Finally, among Wesley's idiosyncrasies and personal faults, being myopic in his approach and application of the Word of God made him prone to being pugnacious about the Bible in his ministry (although others would merely call him arrogant, opinionated, and unrealistic). It is easy to see how much trouble this attribute caused him, historically. However, as Robert Wall comments, for Wesley, "The Bible was always the one book close at hand, an indispensable auxiliary of the Spirit's formative work throughout his life and gospel ministry."[4] The supreme value that Wesley held for scripture and the Good News definitely came at a price for Wesley, but his relationship with God in Jesus Christ was that hidden treasure in the field, that pearl of great value, that he gladly gave all to obtain.[5]

Controversy is nothing new in life to those who dare to stand up for their principles, and Wesley lived his life, much like his religion, with authenticity in mind. Perhaps his youthful escape from a fiery death motivated him to live every day like it could be the last. Perhaps it was a mature, intellectual honest response to his youthful arrogance, ignorance, and spiritual clumsiness. Perhaps it was his conversion experience at Aldersgate that "clearly gave him a confidence and a passion that set him free to explore the full force of the preached Word."[6] What is evident is that Wesley used his life experiences to expand his heart and not shrink in bitterness and pessimism.

Innumerable scholars have tried to fully grasp what happened to Wesley at Aldersgate. Arnett remarks that though Wesley had been religious his entire life, "The true core of the man had been untouched."[7] He had not undergone any real change or renewal

---

4. Wall, "Wesley as Biblical Interpreter," 113.
5. See Matthew 13:44–46.
6. Abraham, "Wesley as Preacher," 100.
7. Arnett, 14.

in his life. He was still controlled by sin, the flesh, and his humanity. However, after his conversion at Aldersgate, Wesley's heart had received "a divine touch and assurance."[8] He was a changed man, freed by the grace and presence of God in his heart. Countering this, Rose states, "Aldersgate was a new beginning in Wesley's spiritual pilgrimage"[9] for Wesley had "moved from a self-centered to a God-centered spiritual universe."[10]

Dayton considers Wesley's joy to be something attainable even to Christians in the modern world. He states, "We seek not the external phenomena but an inner, heart-warming, transforming experience."[11] Thus, successfully complete a spiritual journey like Wesley's requires a whole-hearted admission that all our struggles must be answered in obedient faith to God. Despite scholarly opinion, the result of Wesley's spiritual renewal and biblical approach was the embrace of methodology that is just as impactful today as it was two hundred years ago.

In reading Wesley's words, it is easy to be both drawn and confused by his assertions. Wesley is spot-on in his conviction that there is no place or value for hypocrisy and contrivance in genuine Christianity. A person who professes to love God should respond to God in ways that clearly demonstrate positive personal feelings for Him. Likewise, if believers are to take on the name of Christ, then purity of heart, mind, and soul should be permanently at the top of every Christian's to-do list (especially with Jesus as our model). As Wesley writes in *From Almost to Altogether*, "And he [a Believer] has power over both outward and inward sin, even from the moment he is justified."[12] In Wesley's mind, if one could totally devote oneself to God, he or she could attain the perfected Christian spiritual state.

On the other hand, many consider Wesley's expectations for Christian holiness unrealistic (at least as so far experienced and

---

8. Ibid., 16.
9. Rose, 21.
10. Ibid., 24.
11. Dayton, 31.
12. Wesley, *From Almost to Altogether*, 80.

perceived in Christian history) and dangerous, theologically. In *A Plain Account of Christian Perfection*, Wesley plainly states, "Christians are saved in this world from all sin, from all unrighteousness; that they are now in such a sense perfect, as not to commit sin, and to be freed from evil thoughts and evil tempers."[13] Such a proclamation invites critical inspection and poignant questions, both in Wesley's era and into the postmodern era.

If one can become perfected, is there anymore need for Jesus? And, furthermore, through simple observation, it seems that no flawless Christians exist or have existed, except "perfected" in the saving love and sacrifice of Christ. Even the Apostle John, in his first epistle, seems to challenge Wesley's suggestion of Christian Perfection—"If we say that we have no sin, we deceive ourselves and the truth is not in us" (1 John 1:8). Of course, John's message is clear and concise. People who claim to be Christians, but do not reflect the light or love or truth of God, are simply not Christians, but those who walk with/in the love and truth of God have a perfected relationship with God and each other.

Wesley would whole-heartedly agree that " . . . a person filled with the love of God is still liable to these involuntary transgressions."[14] Such concerns and questions are important, but Wesley would argue that perfect sanctification is in the will and not in the performance. He carefully writes in *A Plain Account of Christian Perfection*, "Therefore, it is as natural for a man to mistake as to breathe; and he can no more live without the one than without the other: consequently, no man is able to perform the service which the Adamic law requires."[15] Yet, he then goes on to state,

> I know many that love God with all their heart. He is their one desire; and they are continually happy in Him. They love their neighbor as themselves. They feel as sincere, fervent, constant a desire for the happiness of every man, good or bad, friend or enemy, as for their own. They

---

13. Wesley, *A Plain Account of Christian Perfection*, 27–28.
14. Ibid., 54.
15. Ibid., 79.

Theological Reflections

rejoice evermore, pray without ceasing, and in everything give thanks. Their souls are continually streaming up to God, in holy joy, prayer, and praise. This is a point of fact; and this is plain, sound, Scripture experience.[16]

In other words, people are permitted to be fallible, although as Christians, they are exhorted to follow Christ's example of perfect love.

Holiness and perfection must be characteristics to be theoretically strived for in the Christian life—for not only do they please God, they also show sincere devotion to him and heart-felt commitment to his good and holy ways. As Rebekah Miles states,

> Religion and happiness, then, are always one; their two parts or branches—love of God and love of neighbor—are indivisible. To choose half of this one religion and one happiness, *either* the love of God *or* love of neighbor, is to lose the whole. This one happiness is the heart of Wesley's ethic.[17]

The success of Wesley's assertions rested upon the possibility of an undivided heart, though, of total desire to dwell in God's love; moreover, Wesley makes it clear that there are no "half-Christians."[18]

Once saved, followers of Christ are fundamentally changed and, therefore, faithful lives should demonstrate it. Total adoration and total surrendering of our will to God can bring about "Christian Perfection," although humanity's fallen nature frequently limits righteous performance. As Vickers writes,

> Although Wesley believed that humans were created in the moral image of God, so that holiness, justice, and goodness reigned in their hearts, he also taught that humans were made in the natural image of God. By this he meant that God created individuals with a liberty to choose whether they would go on obeying the moral law within or whether they would reject it.[19]

16. Ibid., 84.
17. Miles, "Happiness, Holiness, and the Moral Life," 208.
18. Wesley, *A Plain Account of Christian Perfection*, 10.
19. Vickers, 194.

Such limitations, however, are one-sided based on Wesleyan thought (and many Calvinists would agree with this conclusion).

Through human efforts, loving God and loving one's neighbor is difficult, but with the enabling power that comes by being filled with the Spirit of Jesus Christ, and with surrender to trust and obey in God, Christian Perfection is attainable. Thus, Maddox states, "The enduring stress of Wesley's doctrine of Christian perfection, drawn from . . . various sources, was the potential triumph of God's grace and the power of a wholehearted love of God and neighbor to displace all lesser loves and to overcome the remains of sin."[20] Believers can live and respond as Jesus did in the Bible (and as the Bible encourages its readers to do, numerous times).

Such a conclusion not only is Wesleyan; it is also quite evidential. Wesley was, to the end, a man of one book—*the Bible*, and one message—the Good News. In his sermons, Wesley clarified this position, stating,

> Thus, everyone that is holy is, in the Scripture sense, perfect. Yet, we may, lastly, observe, that neither in this respect is there any absolute perfection on earth. There is no perfection of degrees, as it is termed; none which does not admit of a continual increase. So that how much soever any man has attained, or in how high a degree soever he is perfect, he hath still need to "grown in grace," and daily to advance in the knowledge and love of God his Saviour.[21]

The Bible is not an end to itself; it is the divinely spoken path to God's holy embrace. Its main goal is to provide humanity with God's beckoning gift of truth and love to affect personal salvation- and sanctification.

Unto his death bed, Wesley was focused solely on the Bible and its quintessential message—the Good News. Scripture repeatedly shows God crying out for his people to direct their daily lives in holy love for him and each other. The Apostle Paul says it well in 1 Timothy 6:11–12 when he writes, "But you, man of God,

---

20. Maddox and Chilcote, *A Plain Account of Christian Perfection*, 21.
21. Wesley, "Sermon XL—On Christian Perfection," 408.

flee from all this, and pursue righteousness, godliness, faith, love, endurance and gentleness. Fight the good fight of the faith. Take hold of the eternal life to which you were called when you made your good confession in the presence of many witnesses." Perfect unity, perfect love in the Spirit can be attained when Christians open their hearts to Christ Jesus and submit their wills to God. Ultimately, this is the one great truth that Wesley sought to explain and celebrate in his 52 *Standard Sermons*.

Afterword

DR. JOHN S. KNOX has written of Wesley, "He applied his life to his theology."[1] No more poignant summary can be made of the sermons of the Rev. John Wesley than to say that he lived the words that he preached. Trained as a minister, one could argue that the seeds of his conversion at Aldersgate were planted in the seas of the North Atlantic. During his voyage across the Atlantic Ocean, Wesley, the chaplain and priest, witnessed the courageous faith of his Moravian companions in the midst of the storm. As he compared his own fears with their unwavering hope in the face of death, he began to doubt the depths of his personal Christian faith. These fears and Wesley's honest ownership of his humanity birthed a great practical theology that is artfully presented in *John Wesley's 52 Standard Sermons: An Annotated Summary*.

Wesley's ministry took him thousands of miles on horseback with the passion to communicate the Christian message to who would listen. For Wesley, theology needed to be tempered by the practical life. As a chaplain, I, too, have been stirred by the faith of others in the midst of the storm. While traveling across the globe, preaching in diverse places and cultures, I have learned that theology needs to introduce the truth of God to the reality of one's brokenness. Knox's work handily introduces the message of Wesley to

1. See chapter 4, "Theological Reflections."

the Christian reader, and reveals an evangelistic and discipleship message that is still relevant today.

Our Postmodern culture needs to discover what it means to be and live as Christians in a world that is radically changing. Wesley's sermons and his productive method therein provide answers that will address the contemporary audience and its dilemmas. While I am compelled by the message of Wesley, I am also inspired to learn more about its implementation through small groups and praxis.

This book provides a wonderfully succinct and clear analysis of Wesley's preaching. I am left with renewed hope that Christ-centered preaching can indeed change the world. For the pastor and theologian seeking to discover the core of Wesley's life and teaching, this book serves as an excellent primer.

Rev. David R. Leonard
Masters of Divinity, George Fox Seminary
Board Certified Chaplain

Glossary

American Revolutionary War: The battle for independence and region autonomy between the thirteen American Colonies (Delaware, Pennsylvania, New Jersey, Georgia, Connecticut, Massachusetts Bay, Maryland, South Carolina, New Hampshire, Virginia, New York, North Carolina, and Rhode Island/Providence Plantations) and the British Empire (1775-1783).

Anglican Church: See Church of England.

Band: A voluntary weekly meeting of an intimate homogenous group of Methodists to share and confess their spiritual struggles and victories.

Calvinism: The school of theological thought begun by Jean Calvin in the 1500s (and thereafter promoted by his followers) that coupled the Reformation leader Martin Luther's doctrinal position on justification with a austere understanding of predestination to explain the soteriology of saints and sinners.

Charity Schools: As with Kingswood School, John Wesley established several schools for the poor in Bristol, London, and Newcastle to help improve both their education and standard of living.

Glossary

Christian Perfection: A theoretical Christian state wherein the true Christian's whole heart and mind are so attuned to God that his or her will is now ultimately God's—thus, enabling perfection in thought and deed—and this loving devotion is the substance and foundation for all Christian behavior.

Church of England: With historical roots back to the sixth century, CE, the official founding of this branch of Christianity was the result of a schism between King Henry VIII and Pope Clement VII wherein the monarch usurped the role of the pope, and the church became Protestant in doctrine but remained Catholic-like in liturgy.

Class Meeting: A mandatory weekly Methodist meeting wherein members would tithe and discuss their spiritual progress and public Christian deeds.

Deism: A detached form of spiritual belief wherein God exists but does not interfere with human activities.

Dissenters: Various Protestant religious groups (Adamites, Anabaptists, Barrowists, Diggers, Jacobites, Levellers, Lollards, Ranters, Mugbletonians, etc.) that sought to separate from the Church of England.

Egalitarian: The principle that all people, regardless of race, gender, or religion, are equal and thus deserve equal rights under the law and in society.

Enthusiasm: In Britain, a negative term for those of Protestant personal zeal for their religious cause who acted strongly upon their faith, especially in public.

Eucharist: The sacraments of bread and wine shared between believers to remember, represent, and/or symbolize Jesus' words at the Last Supper and his death upon the Cross for all sinners.

Great Awakening: A revivalist movement started in New England in 1730 that swept southward through the other Ameri-

Glossary

can colonies that promoted a return to their Puritan roots and three main concepts of renewed spirituality (terror of the law to sinners, the unmerited grace of God, and new birth in Jesus Christ).

Half-Christians: According to John Wesley, these are people who look like Christians, who do good works, but whose hearts are not driving their behavior or attitude.

Holy Club: A spiritual club begun at Oxford University by Charles Wesley that followed a rigid regimen to improve upon spiritual health and Christian activism.

Homo Unius Libri: Latin for "A man of one book."

Industrial Revolution: An eighteenth-century movement in England that transformed the traditional agrarian lifestyle through the emergence and dominance of new industry and machine manufacturing.

Justification: The Christian notion of healing one's eternal relationship with God presumably at the moment of conversion.

Kingswood School: One of John Wesley's new schools that he established which was renown for its strict educational standards, discipline, and purposeful combination of academics with religion.

Moravian Brethren: Like other branches of Pietism (Halle, Reformed, Radical), this group of Christians sought to revive the church through personal spiritual renewal, and emphasized personal, pragmatic holiness along with authentic, experiential faith.

Non-conformists: Similar to the Dissenters, these were non-Anglican church bodies (Baptists, Congregationalists, Free Churches, Methodists, Presbyterians, Puritans, Quakers, Unitarians, etc.) who advocated religious liberty over state religious authoritarianism.

Glossary

Ordination: A sacrament or ordinance of the church ecclesiology where holy orders are conferred upon a candidate.

Penitent Society: A Methodist group that met mainly on Saturday nights whose main focus was mainstreaming others into the faith, and dealing with severe problems of spiritual and carnal backsliding (such as alcoholism).

Pietism: A Protestant Christian movement that emphasized personal, pragmatic holiness along with embracing scripture as the chief means of renewal, acting kindly and properly in controversial matters, utilizing the priesthood of all believers, and ensuring that sermons were both evangelistic and focused on the love of God for all humanity.

Prevenient Grace: The theological idea that the Holy Spirit is present and active in every person's life going before to positively influence their decisions concerning Christian faith or rejection.

Puritans: English Calvinists who wished to "purify" the Church by returning to a more biblically-centered religion, they put more emphasis on sobriety, scripture, simple lifestyles, and proper Sabbath etiquette.

Quadrilateral: A post-Wesleyan definition of his methodology of cultivating personal spiritual growth, which focused on scripture, tradition, reason, and experience.

Sanctification: Being made like Christ and/or the process of becoming more holy or perfectly righteous, typically over a person's lifetime.

Select Society: Although democratic, this Methodist group focused on the needs and training of leaders in the Methodist Movement through exercises in Christian Perfection, improvement of their particular talents, and Christian ethics.

Glossary

United Societies: According to Wesley, these groups' main goals were to do no harm, to avoid evil of all sorts, to do good of every possible sort, to observe the ordinances of God (including public worship), and to embrace scripture in ministry and sanctification.

Recommended Reading

Primary Sources

Coke, Thomas. *The Letters of Dr. Thomas Coke*, John A. Vickers, Ed. Nashville, TN: Abingdon, 2013.
Olleson, Philip. *Samuel Wesley: The Man and His Music*. Suffolk, UK: Boydell, 2003.
Outler, Albert C. and Richard P. Heitzenrater, eds. *John Wesley's Sermons: An Anthology*. Nashville, TN: Abingdon, 1991.
Potts, J. Manning. *The Journal and Letters of Francis Asbury*. Nashville, TN: Abingdon, 1958.
Wesley, Charles. *Charles Wesley: A Reader*, John R. Tyson, ed. New York, NY: Oxford University, 1989.
Wesley, John. *A Plain Account of Christian Perfection*. Kansas City, MO: Beacon Hill, 1966.
———. *Explanatory Notes Upon the New Testament: (Fully Formatted For E-Readers)*. North Yorkshire, U.K.: Hargreaves, 2014.
———. *Explanatory Notes Upon the Old Testament: (Fully Formatted For E-Readers)*. North Yorkshire, U.K.: Hargreaves, 2014.
———. *From Almost to Altogether: Sermons on Christian Discipleship*. USA, Seedbed, 2015.
———. *How to Pray: The Best of John Wesley*. Uhrichsville, OH: Barbour, 2008.
———. *John Wesley's Commentary on the Bible*. Grand Rapids, MI: Zondervan, 1990.
———. *The Journal of the Rev. John Wesley*. U.S.A.: TheClassics.us, 2013.
———. *The Question: What is an Arminian? Answered. By a Lover of Free Grace*. UK: Hargreaves, 2014.

Recommended Reading

———. *Wesley's 52 Standard Sermons: as He Approved Them*, N. Burwash, ed. Salem, OH: Schmul, 1988.

Wesley, John and Charles Wesley. *A Collection of Hymns for the Use of the People Called Methodists*. Charleston, SC: Nabu, 2011.

Whitefield, George. *Sermons of George Whitefield*, Lee Gatiss, ed. Wheaton, IL: Crossway, 2012.

Bibliography

Abraham, William J. "Wesley as Preacher." In *The Cambridge Companion to John Wesley*, Randy Maddox and Jason Vickers, eds. 98–112. New York, NY: Cambridge, 2010.
Archive.org. "Preface." In *Wesley's Second Oxford Journal*. 1729. Online: https://archive.org/stream/a613690401wesluoft/a613690401wesluoft_djvu.txt
Arnett, William M. "How Aldersgate Affected Wesley." In *Methodism's Aldersgate Heritage*. 14–16. Nashville, TN: Methodist Evangelistic Materials, 1964.
Baker, Frank, ed. "Letters." In *The Works of John Wesley*, Bicentennial Edition, Vol. 25. Nashville, TN: Abingdon, 1980.
Bartleby.com. "A Man of One Book." In *English Prose*, Vol. IV, Henry Craik, ed. New York, NY: The Macmillan Company, 1916. Online: http://www.bartleby.com/209/750.html.
Body, Alfred H. *John Wesley and Education*. London: Epworth, 1936.
Busenitz, Nathan. "John Wesley's Failed Marriage." Online: http://thecripplegate.com/john-wesleys-failed-marriage/.
CCEL.org. "The Earl of Desmond's Castle." Online: http://www.ccel.org/ccel/wesley/journal.vi.xvi.i.html.
CCEL.org. *The Journal of the Rev. John Wesley*. Online: https://www.ccel.org/ccel/wesley/journal.i.html.
CCEL.org. "The Last Year of the Journal." Online: http://www.ccel.org/ccel/wesley/journal.vi.xx.xxii.html?highlight=my,strength,likewise,now,quite,forsook,me#highlight.
CCEL.org. "Wesley's Terrible Ride." Online: http://www.ccel.org/ccel/wesley/journal.vi.xvii.ii.html?highlight=my,generally,preaching,at,five,in,the,morning,one,of,most,healthy,exercises,world#highlight.
Chiles, Robert. *Scriptural Christianity: A Call to John Wesley's Disciples*. U.S.A.: Francis Asbury, 1989.
Collins, Kenneth J. *A Real Christian: The Life of John Wesley*. Nashville, TN: Abingdon, 1989.

BIBLIOGRAPHY

———. *John Wesley: A Theological Journey*. Nashville, TN: Abingdon, 2003.

———. "Wesley's Life and Ministry." In *The Cambridge Companion to John Wesley*, Randy Maddox and Jason Vickers, eds. 43–59. New York, NY: Cambridge, 2010.

Comsource.org. "A Calm Address to the American Colonies" (London, 1775). Online: http://www.consource.org/document/a-calm-address-to-our-american-colonies-by-john-wesley-1775/.

Corbett-Hemeyer, Julia. *Religion in America*. New York, NY: Routledge, 2016.

Curtis, A.K. "A Gallery of Family, Friends and Foes." *Christian History* 2, no. 1 (1983) 7–12.

Curtis, A.K. "John Wesley and Women." *Christian History* 2, no. 1 (1983) 25–27.

———. "Revival and Revolution." *Christian History* 2, no. 1 (1983) 7–9, 34.

———. "What is Pietism?" *Christian History* 5, no. 2 (1986) 3.

Dallimore, Arnold A. *Susanna Wesley: The Mother of John & Charles Wesley*. Grand Rapids: Baker, 1993.

Dayton, Wilber T. "Aldersgate Answers Man's Needs." In *Methodism's Aldersgate Heritage*. 30–31. Nashville, TN: Methodist Evangelistic Materials, 1964.

Dunning, H. Ray. *Reflecting the Divine Image: Christian Ethics in Wesleyan Perspective*. Downers Grove, IL: InterVarsity, 1998.

Durnbaugh, Donald. "The Flowering of Pietism in the Garden of America." *Christian History* 5, no. 2 (1986) 23–27.

Field, David N. "The Unrealized Ethical Potential of the Methodist Theology of Prevenient Grace." *Hervormde Teologiese Studies* 71, no. 1 (2015) 1–8.

Gonzalez, Justo. *The History of Christianity*, Vol 1 and Vol. 2. San Francisco: HarperSanFrancisco, 1985.

———. "Wesley, John (1703–91)." In *An Introductory Dictionary of Theology and Religious Studies*, Orlando O. Espin and James B. Nickoloff, eds. 1483. Collegeville, MN: Liturgical, 2007.

Green, Roger J. "1738 John & Charles Wesley Experience Conversions." Online: http://www.christianitytoday.com/history/issues/issue-28/1738-john-charles-wesley-experience-conversions.html.

Halliday, F.E. *England: A Concise History*. New York, NY: Thames & Hudson, 1995.

Hildebrandt, Franz. *Christianity According to the Wesleys*. Michigan: Baker, 1996.

Hurst, J.F. *John Wesley, the Methodist: A Plain Account of His Life and Work*. Whitefish, MT: Kessinger, 2003.

Knox, John. "John Lathrop." In *The Encyclopedia of Christianity in the United States*. 1319. Lanham, MD: Rowman & Littlefield, 2016.

———. *Sacro-Egoism: The Rise of Religious Individualism in the West*. Eugene, OR: Wipf & Stock, 2016.

MacCulloch, Diarmaid. *Christianity: The First Three Thousand Years*. U.S.A.: Penguin, 2009.

Bibliography

Madden, Deborah. "Wesley as Advisor on Health and Healing." In *The Cambridge Companion to John Wesley*, Randy Maddox and Jason Vickers, eds. 176-189. New York, NY: Cambridge, 2010.

Maddox, Randy and Jason Vickers, eds. *The Cambridge Companion to John Wesley*. New York, NY: Cambridge, 2010.

Maddox, Randy and Paul W. Chilcote, eds. *A Plain Account of Christian Perfection*. Kansas City, MO: Beacon Hill, 2015.

Miles, Rebekah L. "Happiness, Holiness, and the Moral Life in John Wesley." In *The Cambridge Companion to John Wesley*, Randy Maddox and Jason Vickers, eds. 207-224. New York, NY: Cambridge, 2010.

Nichols, Joel A. "Religious Liberty in the Thirteenth Colony: Church-State Relations in Colonial and Early National Georgia." *New York University Law Review* 80, no. 6 (December 2005) 1693-1772.

Noll, Mark. *A History of Christianity in the United States and Canada*. Grand Rapids, MI: Eerdmans, 1992.

O'Brien, Glen. "John Wesley, the Uniting Church, and the Authority of Scripture." *Pacifica* 27, no. 2 (2014) 170-183.

Olsen, Roger. *The Story of Christian Theology: Twenty Centuries of Tradition & Reform*. Downers Grove, IL: InterVarsity, 1999.

Outler, Albert C., ed. "An Early Self-Analysis." In *John Wesley*. 41-50. New York, NY: Oxford University, 1964.

Packer, J.L. "Theology on Fire." *Christian History* 8, no. 1 (1994) 32-35.

Pedlar, James. "John Wesley on Predestination." Online: https://jamespedlar.wordpress.com/2012/02/16/john-wesley-on-predestination/.

Rose, Delbert R. "Aldersgate Set Wesley on Fire for God." In *Methodism's Aldersgate Heritage*. 21-24. Nashville, TN: Methodist Evangelistic Materials, 1964.

Shelley, Bruce L. *Church History in Plain Language*. Nashville, TN: Nelson, 1995.

Steiner, Susie. "Top Five Regrets of the Dying." Online: https://www.theguardian.com/lifeandstyle/2012/feb/01/top-five-regrets-of-the-dying.

Towns, Elmer L. "John Wesley and Religious Education." *Articles, Paper* 16 (1970) 318-328.

Townsend, Jim. "The Forgotten Wesley." *Christian History* 10, no. 3 (1991) 6-8.

UMC.org. "Wesleyan Quadrilateral." Online: http://www.umc.org/what-we-believe/wesleyan-quadrilateral.

Vickers, Jason. "Wesley's Theological Emphases." In *The Cambridge Companion to John Wesley*, Randy Maddox and Jason Vickers, eds. 190-206. New York, NY: Cambridge, 2010.

Vickers, John A. "One-man Band: Thomas Coke and the Origins of Methodist Missions." *Methodist History* 34, no. 3 (April 1996) 135.

Wall, Robert W. "Wesley as Biblical Interpreter." In *The Cambridge Companion to John Wesley*, Randy Maddox and Jason Vickers, eds. 113-128. New York, NY: Cambridge, 2010.

Bibliography

Walsh, J.D. "Wesley vs. Whitefield: The Conflict Between the Two Giants of the Eighteenth-century Awakening." *Christian History* 38, no. 2 (1993) 34–37.

Wesley Center Online. "Chapter XIII—In Conference with the Preachers." Online: http://wesley.nnu.edu/john-wesley/john-wesley-the-methodist/chapter-xiii-in-conference-with-the-preachers/.

Wesley Center Online. "Free Grace." *The Sermons of John Wesley—Sermon* 128. Online: https://www.whdl.org/sites/default/files/publications/EN_John_Wesley_128_free_grace.htm.

Wesley, John. *A Plain Account of Christian Perfection*. Kansas City, MO: Beacon Hill, 1966.

———. *From Almost to Altogether: Sermons on Christian Discipleship*. USA, Seedbed, 2015.

———. *How to Pray: The Best of John Wesley on Prayer*. Uhrichsville, OH: Barbour, 2007.

———. *The Question: What is an Arminian? Answered. By a Lover of Free Grace*. UK: Hargreaves, 2014.

———. *Wesley's 52 Standard Sermons: as He Approved Them*. Salem, OH: Schmul, 1988.

Wood, Timothy L. "'That They May Be Free Indeed': Liberty in the Early Methodist Thought of John Wesley and Francis Asbury." *Methodist History* 38, no. 4 (July 2000) 231–241.

52 Standard Sermons Topical Index

Additional Notes

Abstinence	Sermon 27	_____
Altruism	Sermon 49	_____
Amazement	Sermon 45	_____
Application	Sermon 4	_____
Appreciation	Sermon 28, 48	_____
Asleep	Sermon 3	_____
Attacks	Sermon 42	_____
Authenticity	Sermon 16, 24	_____
Awareness	Sermon 36	_____
Belief	Sermon 7	_____
Beneficence	Sermon 34	_____
Bigotry	Sermon 38	_____
Caution	Sermon 31	_____
Charity	Sermon 22	_____
Christ-model	Sermon 48	_____
Commandments	Sermon 25	_____
Complacency	Sermon 3	_____
Conscience	Sermon 15	_____
Contrivance	Sermon 36	_____
Controversy	Sermon 20	_____

52 Standard Sermons Topical Index

Conviction	Sermon 17
Cultivation	Sermon 4
Dangers	Sermon 31
Darkness	Sermon 3, 47
Despair	Sermon 46
Devotion	Sermon 20
Doctrine	Sermon 11, 13
Enlightenment	Sermon 3
Enthusiasm	Sermon 10, 27
Evangelism	Sermon 24
Exclusivity	Sermon 31
Exercise	Sermon 43
Faith	Sermon 1, 2, 5, 14, 30, 35, 43
Fall, the	Sermon 19
False Prophets	Sermon 32
Fasting	Sermon 27
Foolishness	Sermon 33
Freedom	Sermon 8
Fruit	Sermon 32
Fulfillment	Sermon 25
Good Intentions	Sermon 26
Gospel, the	Sermon 35
Grace	Sermon 1, 7, 9, 16
Grief	Sermon 47
Hard-heartedness	Sermon 32
Healing	Sermon 44
Heart	Sermon 7
Heaviness	Sermon 47
Holiness	Sermon 24
Honesty	Sermon 26
Hope	Sermon 18
Humbleness	Sermon 26
Humanity	Sermon 44

52 Standard Sermons Topical Index

Hypocrisy	Sermon 27, 30
Ignorance	Sermon 17, 46
Imputation	Sermon 20
Inspiration	Sermon 39
Intellectual Weakness	Sermon 41
Investment	Sermon 28, 50
Joy	Sermon 12, 23
Judgment	Sermon 15, 30
Justification	Sermon 5, 19, 45
Kingdom	Sermon 7, 51
Law	Sermon 5, 6, 9, 34, 36
Love	Sermon 18, 39, 40
Loyalty	Sermon 29
Manners	Sermon 52
Maturity	Sermon 29
Meekness	Sermon 22
Money	Sermon 50
Morality	Sermon 52
Moral Weakness	Sermon 41
Natural Man	Sermon 9
Nature	Sermon 15
New Birth	Sermon 18, 45
Obedience	Sermon 6
Openness	Sermon 30
Order	Sermon 15
Original Sin	Sermon 44
Patience	Sermon 8
Peacefulness	Sermon 23
Pentecost	Sermon 4
Perfection	Sermon 40
Persecution	Sermon 23
Pride	Sermon 27, 50

52 Standard Sermons Topical Index

Prioritization	Sermon 29
Process	Sermon 35
Protection	Sermon 42
Purity	Sermon 23
Reality	Sermon 9, 28
Regeneration	Sermon 13, 19, 45
Repentance	Sermon 14
Responsibility	Sermon 49
Reverence	Sermon 26
Rewards	Sermon 27
Righteousness	Sermon 6, 20, 22, 25
Satan	Sermon 42
Salvation	Sermon 1, 16, 35, 43
Sanctification	Sermon 40
Scripture	Sermon 11, 13, 43
Self-awareness	Sermon 12
Self-control	Sermon 8, 52
Self-deception	Sermon 33
Self-denial	Sermon 48
Self-protection	Sermon 38
Shallowness	Sermon 33
Sin	Sermon 5, 13, 14, 19, 46
Sincerity	Sermon 12
Spirit	Sermon 10, 11
Spiritual Disease	Sermon 46
Spiritual Health	Sermon 39
Slander	Sermon 49
Snobbery	Sermon 38
Society	Sermon 52
Soul	Sermon 17
Stewardship	Sermon 51
Stumbling Blocks	Sermon 21
Submission	Sermon 48

52 Standard Sermons Topical Index

Supererogation	Sermon 51	_____
Superficiality	Sermon 37	_____
Temptations	Sermon 41, 46	_____
Trial	Sermon 47	_____
True Religion	Sermon 2, 21, 44	_____
Trust	Sermon 29	_____
Truth	Sermon 10	_____
Universal Brotherhood	Sermon 39	_____
Usefulness	Sermon 34	_____
Vanity	Sermon 28	_____
Victory	Sermon 46	_____
Waste	Sermon 50	_____
Way, the	Sermon 7	_____
Wisdom	Sermon 50	_____
Witness	Sermon 11	_____
Worry	Sermon 29	_____
Zeal	Sermon 37	_____

General Index

A Plain Account of Christian Perfection, 21, 80
Aldersgate Street, 78–79
American Colonies, x, 11, 22–24, 26, 87
American Revolutionary War, 22, 24, 87
Anglican Church, x, 1, 6, 15–16, 21, 24–25, 87
Apostle Paul, 76, 82
Arminius, Jacob, 2, 22
Asbury, Francis, 24–25

Band, The, 17, 87

Calvinism/ist, 2, 11, 16, 21–22, 90
Charity Schools, 18, 88
Christian Perfection, 2–3, 15, 66, 80–82, 88
Church of England, 8, 11–13, 16, 21, 24–26, 88
Class Meeting, The, 17, 88
Coke, Thomas, 24–25
Connecticut, Colony of, 11, 87

Deism, 7, 88
Delaware, Colony of, 11, 87

Edwards, Jonathan, 11
Egalitarian, 2, 88
English Law, 24
Enthusiasm, 7, 15, 38, 63–64, 88
Epworth Rectory, 8, 77

Frelinghuysen, Theo, 11
From Almost to Altogether, 79

Georgia, Colony of, 9, 11–14
Great Awakening, x, 3, 11, 89

Half-Christians, 32, 81, 89
Holy Club, x, 9, 89
Holy Spirit, 4, 15, 22, 33–34, 36–37, 43, 45, 77, 90
Homo Unius Libri, vi, 89
Hopkey, Sophey, 14
How to Pray: The Best of John Wesley on Prayer, 22

Industrial Revolution, 6, 25, 89

Jesus, 46–47, 50–51, 66, 78–80, 82–83
Journal of John Wesley, 9–10, 20, 26, 77
Justification, 34

105

General Index

Kingswood School, 18, 88–89
Kirkham, Sally, 10

Maryland, Colony of, 11, 87
Massachusetts, Colony of, 11, 87
Methodist church, 17, 21, 24–26
Moravian Brethren, 12–13, 27, 89
Murray, Grace, 19

New York, Colony of, 11, 87
New Jersey, Colony of, 11, 87
Non-conformist, 6–7, 87

Ordination, 24, 90
Oxford College, 8–10, 77, 89

Penitent Society, The, 17, 90
Pennsylvania, Colony of, 87

Pietism, 13, 89, 90
Prevenient Grace, 2, 90
Puritanism, 6, 11, 16, 23

Quadrilateral, 17, 90

Select Society, The, 17, 90

United Societies, 17, 91

Vasey, Tomas, 24
Vazeille, "Molly" Mary, 19
Virginia, Colony of, 11, 87

Wesley, Samuel, 7
Wesley, Susanna, 7
Wesley, Charles, x, 9, 11–12, 89
Whatcost, Richard, 24

www.ingramcontent.com/pod-product-compliance
Lightning Source LLC
Chambersburg PA
CBHW060404090426
42734CB00011B/2255